HAPPY
DOG

How Busy People Care
for Their Dogs

A Stress-Free
Guide for
All Dog Owners

**By Arden Moore &
Lowell Ackerman, D.V.M.**

A DIVISION OF FANCY PUBLICATIONS
Irvine, California

Ruth Strother, Project Manager
Nick Clemente, Special Consultant
Karla Austin, Editor
Michelle Martinez, Assistant Editor
Designed by Bocu & Bocu

The dogs in this book are referred to as *he* and *she* in alternating chapters.
The photos on pages 15, 16, 18, 19, 22, 45, 90, 95, 100, 111, 116, 132, and 155
are courtesy of comstock.com.
Copyright © 2003 by BowTie™ Press

Library of Congress Cataloging-in-Publication Data
Moore, Arden.
 Happy dog, how busy people care for their dogs : a stress-free guide
for all dog owners / by Arden Moore and Lowell Ackerman.
     p. cm.
Includes bibliographical references (p.   ).
 ISBN 1-931993-02-5 (pbk. : alk. paper)
 1. Dogs. 2. Dogs--Behavior. I. Ackerman, Lowell J. II. Title.
 SF426 .M677 2003
 636.7--dc21

                    2002153044

                    BOWTIE™ PRESS
        A DIVISION OF FANCY PUBLICATIONS
                    3 Burroughs
                Irvine, California 92618

        Printed and Bound in Singapore
            10 9 8 7 6 5 4 3 2 1

★   ★   ★   ★   ★   ★   ★   ★   ★

*I dedicate this book to my wonderful wife, Susan, and my
three incredible children, Nadia, Rebecca, and David, and to our
much-loved Golden retriever Marilyn.*
—LOWELL ACKERMAN, D.V.M.

*I dedicate this book to my best friends, Marcia, Barbara, and Jim;
to my pet-loving siblings, Deb, Karen, and Kevin; to my corgi, Jazz;
and to dog lovers everywhere.*
—ARDEN MOORE

CONTENTS

FOREWORD

If dogs had their way, they would become our faithful four-legged shadows, delightfully mirroring our every footstep. They would accompany us to work, join us on vacation, and be by our side not only every waking moment but every resting one as well. Quite simply, they would be reveling in dog heaven right here on earth. And being the caring, compassionate companions they are, dogs would beg for a second wish (this one for us): They would gleefully erase guilt—that stress-magnifying emotion—from our vocabularies, thoughts, and lives. *Bury guilt,* they would tell us. *It stinks!*

Guilt seems to be a stubborn mainstay in today's society, especially among caring dog owners who are trying to juggle jobs, schooling, travel, and families with spending quality time with their ever-lovin' dogs. As a veteran veterinarian who travels all over the country—and the world—promoting the bond between pets and people, I witness firsthand how guilt takes a taxing toll on folks who are frustrated because they can't spend more time with their dogs. Many of my clients begin their sentences with such phrases as *I wish I had, If only I could,* or *I should have,* lamenting about not sharing more special moments with their canine pals.

Fortunately, grr-eat help has arrived for all worry-weary dog owners. In *Dog Fancy's Happy Dog: How Busy People Care for Their Dogs,* authors Arden Moore and Dr. Lowell Ackerman skillfully tackle this troubling topic—guilt—and offer a wide assortment of on-target solutions that are sure to bring relief and joy to dog owners everywhere. Need to work late tonight? No problem. You have an army of pet allies ready to step in and assist. No time to spend 20 minutes each day reinforcing what you learned from dog obedience class? You'll learn how to incorporate those essential *sit, stay,* and *leave it* commands seamlessly into your daily routine. Not sure what to pack for your dog on your next road trip together? Delight in the story of Maggie, the well-traveled German shepherd dog who has visited 21 states and counting.

Each chapter is loaded with smart solutions for having a howling good time with your dog pal.

Moore and Ackerman spotlight plenty of success stories of dog owners who have learned how to enrich their lives with dogs without a lick of guilt! You'll be inspired by Joe Sporn, who opened the country's first doggy day care center to ease the separation anxiety of his German shepherd dog puppy, Valkyrie. And delight in reading how first-time dog owner Lori Davis can graciously decline unwanted after-work invitations, now that she shares her life with Lacey, a spirited sheltie (Shetland sheepdog).

These and more telling tales serve to motivate and reassure you and other dog owners that yes, you can work, raise a family, and enjoy a win-win partnership with your pet pals.

I heartily invite you to read on, lap up all the great guidance in this book, and watch your layers of guilt magically disappear.

Caring for pets and people,

—Marty Becker, D.V.M.

INTRODUCTION

Are you guilt-ridden each morning you bid bye-bye to your dog and head off to work or school? Do you worry if your dog is getting enough socialization and attention while you work or attend classes sometimes for 10- or 12-hours a day? Do you turn down last minute after-work invitations because you need to get home to walk your dog? Do you worry about finding a place to live that will accept your furry friend? You're in abundant company. Most dog owners love their dogs dearly and pray that they never have to decide between keeping their dogs and taking terrific jobs in places with classified housing ads that read, "No pets allowed."

The majority of dog owners live in homes with zero lot lines or in condominiums, apartments, or townhouses in metropolitan cities and sprawling suburbs. The days of dog lovers providing huge fenced backyards or spacious acreage for their dogs to romp supervised by a homemaker mom are fast disappearing to join other outdated symbols of Americana.

Dogs certainly have come a long way from their early years as descendants of wolves. First domesticated by cave people as worthy hunting partners, dogs have evolved from sleeping outside caves to being revered as gods in ancient Egyptian times to dutifully handling night-watch duties inside barns to guarding livestock and crops for farmers in the twentieth century. Dogs have more recently evolved from backyard protectors to bedroom-blanket stealers, with nary a single complaint lodged from any of us. Their roles have changed from skilled hunters to cherished companions.

People's roles have also evolved. We no longer call ourselves masters. Even the title *owner* is now being replaced in some areas of the country with more enlightened titles such as *guardian* or *companion caretaker*. In 2000, Boulder, Colorado, became the first city in the country to replace all references to animal owners with the phrase *animal guardians* in their municipal codes to encourage people to treat their dogs more like members of the family and less like property. The phrase *pet parent* is now spoken without a hint of embarrassment in many circles.

Corporate America is also changing its view of dogs. More and more companies, big and small, are becoming responsive to the needs and wishes of today's pet-owning consumers. At a recent pet products expo in San Diego, more than five hundred vendors proudly displayed more than 1,500 pet-related products, ranging from nonskid food bowls to the latest in raingear for puddle-seeking poodles. Dogs are gaining the welcome mat at more hotels, shops, fine eateries, and workplaces.

We are making another leap in the evolution of the people-canine bond. More of us are recognizing that dogs don't exist just to serve us; they play direct roles in keeping us healthy—physically, emotionally, and even spiritually. Research has shown that pet ownership increases the survival rate in heart attack patients. A 1995 study, published in the *American Journal of Cardiology*, showed that in patients with heart attacks and irregular heartbeats, less than 1 percent of patients who owned dogs died, compared to 6.5 percent of patients who didn't own a dog. Similarly, a variety of studies have shown that owning a dog can relieve stress and lower blood pressure. The reasons for such benefits may be difficult

to enumerate, but the facts speak for themselves.

Dogs also make great therapists, and there are now many animal assistance therapy dogs at work across the country. Why would a child with behavioral problems and a poor record of response to different counselors open up to a four-legged therapist? We don't know, but it is a joy to behold.

Everyone is celebrating the human-animal bond in one form or another, and our communities and social systems are changing in meaningful ways to accommodate this. More housing that welcomes pets is coming available. There are more hotels, motels, tourist attractions, and even shopping centers that are saying yes to pets. You can now find pet-friendly places on the Internet through such Web sites as www.rentwithpets.com or www.traveldog.com.

Even the laws of the land are changing. Since medieval times, pets have been considered simply as chattel—with no more rights than a sofa or a toaster. That's changing. At least 12 law schools, including Harvard, offer courses in animal law. Stephen Wise, a Boston lawyer and an instructor for the Harvard course, is the author of *Rattling the Cage*, a book that argues for legal rights for animals. He simply acknowledges that the changes seen are just the result of the courts catching up with reality.

If you don't think there have been real changes in the law, just look at the news. While road rage is so common in America that it's almost immune to news coverage, that all changed when a dog was killed in such an incident. In this 2001 road-rage case that sparked a global animal cruelty debate, the jury took only 40 minutes to convict the accused offender of flinging Leo, the bichon frise, to his death. The accused was convicted of felony animal cruelty that had a prison sentence of up to three years. Appalled pet lovers across the nation raised about $120,000 to help find and prosecute the killer. Some law enforcement officials complained that this case garnered more attention than the trial of a serial killer, but most animal protection groups said the case raised needed awareness to address animal cruelty.

No one knows the extent of animal abuse in this country, but the link between domestic violence and animal abuse is becoming more clearly appreciated. Studies show that women in abusive relationships may delay entering a shelter for fear of what may happen if they leave their pets. In response to this crisis, psychologist Frank Ascione of Utah State University compiled *Safe Havens for Pets: Guidelines for Programs Sheltering Pets for Women Who Are Battered*. The Humane Society of the United States (HSUS), as part of its First Strike campaign, has provided research that shows that a large number of cases of intentional animal cruelty involved some form of family violence, whether domestic violence, child abuse, or elder abuse. The HSUS seeks to turn the nation's attention to the connection between abuse toward animals and violence toward people. First Strike is a public awareness campaign aimed at educating pet owners on their legal recourses if their pet is harmed or killed. The campaign also provides workshops that unite social workers, animal protection workers, law officials,

educators, veterinarians, and concerned citizens.

Another pressing matter with direct connections to the reality of today's families is the issue of latchkey children and pets being left alone at home for extended periods. In this book we address different ways of dealing with the situation for dogs, but comparing it to the situation with children is also worthy of consideration. Between 2.5 and 5 million children in America between the ages of 5 and 14 are referred to as latchkey children, kids who care for themselves while their parents are at work. As you might imagine, many of these kids are responsible, feel safe, and do just fine taking care of themselves, but all experts recommend that children under the age of 10 should not be left in these circumstances. The main problem for children left unsupervised and just hanging out is their tendency to get into trouble. They are far more likely to have behavioral problems and give in to negative peer pressures.

While dogs are unlikely to descend into substance abuse as a consequence of being alone, they are more likely to become bored and get into trouble when left unsupervised. That's just a fact. While we promote a guilt-free philosophy to dog ownership, we also stress responsibility and nipping problems in the bud by doing things the right way from the start. More dogs are euthanized for behavioral problems in this country than for all medical problems combined, so don't underestimate what happens when latchkey canines get into trouble.

Blame it on society mores if you wish, but there is no longer a demographically stable American family unit. That standard unit of a mother, a father, and 2.3 children has gone the way of the family farm and the station wagon. In the old days the kids went to school, Dad went to work, and Mom stayed home to tend the house and care for the family dog. For the most part, for better or for worse, those days are gone. These days, households may feature two wage earners with no one home during the day, as well as single wage earners solely responsible for caring for a household with pets and/or kids. Accordingly, just as family members now share household duties more equitably, they also need to make different arrangements for the dog's care. Don't worry. We have a lot of great tips throughout the book for all the different circumstances in which you may find yourself taking responsibility for the care of a dog.

Don't be dismayed that taking responsible care of your dog means giving up your on-the-go lifestyle. We're here to help! There has never been a better time to indulge yourself and your canine companion in a thoroughly enjoyable and mutually beneficial cross-species relationship.

For you on-the-go dog lovers who are determined to manage a life as well as cultivate a caring and committed canine relationship, this is your time. As the name implies, *Dog Fancy's Happy Dog: How Busy People Care for Their Dogs* is loaded with practical tips, savvy solutions, and emotion-generating stories to help you raise a dog indoors without a lick of guilt! Learn how your boss can be one of your best dog allies. Discover the safest—and most fun—ways to travel with your dog. Find out how your dog can actually save you from a blind date that is getting worse by the moment. Our goal is to help you delete guilt from your vocabulary and your mind—or at least transform the word into a new, positive acronym that stands for:

Great

Useful

Intelligent

Loving

Tactics

Adapt this new definition of G-U-I-L-T, and you will never feel terrible about not being able to spend 24-7 with your canine chum.

Paws up!

How Much We Love Our Dogs!

A recent national survey conducted by the American Animal Hospital Association revealed among dog owners:

- ✔ 87 percent happily include their dogs in holiday celebrations;
- ✔ 84 percent view themselves as pet parents;
- ✔ 75 percent consider their dogs to be smart or even geniuses;
- ✔ 65 percent admit that they sing or dance for their dogs regularly;
- ✔ 63 percent say they celebrate their dogs' birthdays;
- ✔ 53 percent do not hesitate to take time off work to care for their sick dogs;
- ✔ 44 percent report that they have taken their dogs to work on occasion;
- ✔ 43 percent proudly display photos of their dogs at their workstation.

CHAPTER I

* * * * * * * * *

THE NATURE OF DOGS AND PEOPLE

* * * * * * * * *

You head out for work in the early morning and, if you're lucky, you return home as the sun is setting. The time your dog spends home alone can range from 6 to 12 hours— or more. Do you ever stop to wonder exactly what your dog does during this solitary time? Do her actions explain those mysterious toll calls that keep appearing on your telephone bill? Is she busy on your computer, doggedly searching for pet-related specials on the Internet but unable to act without a credit card? Does she secretly invite the neighborhood dogs over for a canine party?

If you are curious about what your dog is doing in your absence, welcome to the new millennium. You can set up a Web cam and view your dog's activities in your abode from just about anywhere in the world. Or you can set up a nanny cam and tape your dog's antics for later viewing. However, what you are likely to see is a fair amount of downtime when you are not around. The biggest time-consuming activity among dogs is sleep. Some dogs by nature snooze several hours during the day. After all, when their owners are not around, what could possibly be that exciting? You can spice up your dog's day by

Setting up a Web cam can enable you to see what your dog is doing while you are not at home.

By nature some dogs snooze several hours a day.

putting the television and/or VCR on a timer to play while you're not there, or play audiotapes and CDs that provide calming canine sounds. Whatever you do will surely be appreciated, but the very best option is to get your dog accustomed to a schedule and do your best to adhere to it.

We would like to take the mystery out of your home-alone dog so that you can brush aside any pangs of guilt. But first, let's address what makes dogs tick. Yes, it is true that dogs are social creatures who prefer our company to being alone. In fact, they often prefer being with us to being with members of their own species. Talk about your animal magnetism!

Although dogs' ancient ancestors were almost certainly wolves, in the domestication process we have bred a lot of the wildness out of our canine companions. In fact, as part of domestication, we have selected for juvenile, or puppylike, qualities, a process known as pedomorphosis. That helps explain why today's adult dogs still possess a lot of puppy personality and why canines of all ages crave the direction of a dominant family member.

In the wild, wolves abide by a prominent social order, with alpha males and females at the top of the pecking order. In our human-pet relationship, we assume the role of the alpha leader, and that allows us to set a lot of the rules that must be followed on our turf. Fortunately for us, dogs appreciate a strict social order, and they are much happier abdicating leadership to us. For us, it's important to set rules that are clear and consistent to our dogs. Often, doggy "misdeeds" are the result of people being inconsistent in communications.

One of the most common and troubling behavior problems seen today is separation anxiety, which arises when a dog feels abandoned when left alone.

That is to be anticipated when a dog is purchased, played with nonstop for several days, and then left alone at home for long periods of time. The result is often incessant barking, the chewing of personal items, and lapses in house-training. What else would you expect? The dog, comforted by all the company during the first few days in the home, is simply reacting to this drastic change in the daily routine.

A dog with separation anxiety chews things, barks incessantly, and has lapses in house-training.

While there are prescription medications to treat separation anxiety, certainly our goal is not to abandon a dog at home and then drug her so that she doesn't realize it. Before you start requesting drugs from your veterinarian, take a step back to assess the situation and see if there isn't an easier way to avoid the problem in the first place. Medications work satisfactorily only when they are coupled with a program that solves the underlying problem—and that underlying problem is rarely an inherent canine anxiety disorder.

The Guilty Truth About Dogs and People

While it is tempting to anthropomorphize your dog, giving human reasons for misbehaviors, get over yourself. Your dog is a dog, not a four-legged, hairy person. Your dog didn't urinate on the carpet to teach you a lesson for making picnic plans with your new beau that didn't involve her. She didn't chew your new shoes because you forgot to pick up her favorite treats when you did your shopping. And she doesn't resent you because your boss gave you a raise that came with more work responsibilities. Often the reasons for doggy misdeeds are boredom, an overtaxed bladder, and a need for appropriate chew toys of her own.

A dog who shows submission and fear bows her head and puts her ears back.

Dogs don't feel guilt. That's right. That's an emotion only people are "fortunate" to feel, according to Larry Lachman, Psy.D., an animal behavior consultant in Carmel, California, who holds a doctorate in clinical psychology. "Guilt is self-reflective. You know you did wrong. Dogs do not have the brain ability to do that type of abstract thinking," says

An animal behavior consultant can help you develop a strong relationship with your dog.

starts with truly understanding how a dog thinks. "When people say, 'I know my dog knows he wasn't supposed to pee on the sofa. When I come home, he bows his head and looks away. His ears are back and he won't come near me. I know he feels guilty,'" says Dr. Lachman, "in reality, the dog has associated the pee with his pack leader—you—coming home being angry, which he can tell by your voice, body odor, eye stare, and stance. Your dog is doing an instinctive wolf submissive response so that you, his pack leader, won't bite him in the neck and kill him. For him, it's pure submission and fear, not an ounce of guilt."

The Good and Bad About Guilt

One part of understanding the human-dog bond is to understand the dog's nature. Equally important in building better people-pet connections comes in analyzing our emotions. Keep in mind that guilt is a double-sided emotion: it can bring out the best and spotlight the worst—in all of us. Dr. Lachman views guilt as a great motivator when it is used to keep us doing what we know is right and when it helps us stay responsible to ourselves, family, friends, coworkers,

Dr. Lachman. "But I do believe that the emotions of fear and submission are instinctive responses hardwired into a dog's nervous system. Those are two emotions that dogs are capable of experiencing."

Dr. Lachman helps dog owners develop stronger relationships with their canine companions. It all and dogs. "If guilt prompts people to consistently care for their dogs by providing them with adequate nutritional, medical, social, and exercise needs, then I'm all for guilt," says Dr. Lachman.

A little guilt also works effectively in building pet responsibility in children. Dr. Lachman urges parents to instill empathy for pets in their children so they can understand their dogs' needs. Remind your child that when he or she is sick or bangs a knee from a bicycle spill, you are there to wipe away the tears and provide relief. The child can give that same care and comfort to the family dog. "Tell your children that just like them, your dog has fears, and feels lonely at times," says Dr. Lachman. "Dogs need exercise, fresh water, fresh food, obedience, and regular walks. They rely on everyone in the family to feel happy, content, and secure. We are their guardians."

Dr. Lachman used to feel guilty when his busy schedule kept him away from Max, his beloved flat-coated retriever. Then, one day, he took out a piece of paper and divided it into three columns with the headings of My Needs, My Dog's Needs, and Our Needs. In each, he wrote down 8 to 10 items.

Through making a list, you can learn to identify your needs, which may include dating twice a week,

working out three times a week at the local gym, or enrolling in a cooking class. Write down 8 to 10 of your favorite activities. For your dog's needs, you need to think like your dog. What does she enjoy doing? Possible activities to list may include being run three times a week, going to the doggy park on the weekend, or being walked on different routes so she can explore—and sniff—new territories. For the final list, Our Needs, jot down several activities that you and your dog enjoy doing in tandem. They

Make a list of your dog's needs so that you can be sure to meet them.

Bike riding and being outdoors is something you and your dog can enjoy doing together.

can include having your dog be your pal when you need to run quick errands, arranging to spend the day hiking or camping with your dog at a canine-friendly park, enrolling in an agility training class, or double-dating with someone who owns a dog. "The key is to strive for balance in your life," says Dr. Lachman. "Writing these lists helps create a written contract between you and your dog. By doing a few items on the list each week, you will be able to reduce stress caused by guilt and feel much happier."

Today, Dr. Lachman is guilt-free when it comes to Max because he has pet allies who come in and walk Max or pet sit when he needs to work late or travel. And Dr. Lachman makes sure to schedule quality, interactive time each week with Max.

Accept Your Role as the Alpha Leader

Much of the success in your relationship with your dog is remembering that you reign as the alpha leader in your household. You make the plans, and your dog follows gleefully. If you don't affix

Your dog can learn to adapt to your schedule.

human emotions and thought processes to your dog, you'll both be a lot happier with the relationship. Dogs thrive on consistency and seek routines.

Your dog's life is completely intertwined with yours, and her schedule is entirely dependent on yours. If you work a nine-to-five job, it isn't long before your dog begins to anticipate that you leave at a certain time in the morning and return at approximately the same time each evening. She picks up the cues: jingling the car keys, picking up the briefcase, and even your style of dress. Dogs are savvy enough to know that their caretakers normally dress differently during the week than on weekends. This savviness can explain why some dogs sometimes sleep in longer on weekends: they learn that owners wake up later on Saturday and Sunday mornings. Dogs learn to plan their day around their people's routines.

While your dog may not be able to read the time on your clock, her internal clock is quite able to discern the time that you are anticipated home. So just prior to your typical arrival time, your dog is attuned to listen for those telltale signs—the sound of the garage door opening, the elevator chime, footsteps on the stairs, or keys in the lock (depending on where you live). This is the most important part of your dog's day, the time for greetings, for being acknowledged, and perhaps for being fed and given a toilet break. So imagine how stressful it is when you are two hours late getting home from work or you come home feeling cranky or too tired to be the alpha leader. It's your dog's worst nightmare.

Prior to your typical arrival home, your dog listens for any sound of you.

Enlist the Aid of Others

Now back to using a little psychology on your dog. The secret to getting your dog to buy into your schedule is to do it gradually, enlisting the help of friends or professionals when necessary, and to build on the bond of trust that develops between you and your furry best friend. It's not as difficult as you might imagine.

Fortunately, being a dog owner in the twenty-first century does not mean that you can't work or have a social life. It just means that you have responsibility for a creature who thinks that you are a god and lives to please you. That's an awesome responsibility, but it's also great for your self-esteem. Don't abuse the reverence, and you'll both do just fine.

In reality, meeting the needs of your dog is the easiest relationship task that you'll ever have. After all, if you really need to stay late at the office to get work done or to go out with that certain someone,

Many dogs take naps while their owner is away.

If a dog had a daily planner, here is what might appear on her agenda:

- ✓ Wake up owner at 6:30 A.M. with a cold, wet nose to the forehead.
- ✓ Make a bathroom walk and be sure to mark the oak tree down the block to let the other dogs in the neighborhood know I've been there.
- ✓ Usher my owner out the door with a friendly woof! and plenty of tail-wagging bye-byes.
- ✓ Head for my bed in the living room and take a much-needed snooze until 10:30 A.M.
- ✓ Wake up in time to bark at the postal carrier delivering mail.
- ✓ Take a slow walk around the house to check out everything.
- ✓ Drink some water and gnaw on my chew toy for a while.
- ✓ Leap on my owner's bed, fuss with the bedspread, and take another two-hour nap.
- ✓ Wake up and spend part of the afternoon looking out the living room window at the passing cars and barking at the birds and squirrels. Be sure to smear the window with my moist nose.
- ✓ Take a well-deserved late afternoon nap to be energized when my owner returns.

Timing Pet Adoptions

Separation anxiety can result when you do not train your dog to anticipate your absences. When you purchase a dog on a Friday night and play with her all weekend, she has no clue that this undivided attention will end abruptly on Monday morning. On Sunday, you devoted the entire day to bonding with her. On Monday, you're suddenly a no-show for eight hours or more. If you have kids, it's a double whammy when you go to work and the dog's play-mates suddenly disappear to go to school.

And while we're on the subject of timing, let's dispel the myth that the best time to adopt a puppy is when you're on a long vacation or during the holiday season. The holidays are the wrong time to bring a furry friend into your family. During this time, the home environment is anything but typical and is often filled with stress, with everyone dashing here and there. "A puppy or a newly adopted dog needs to be viewed as a living creature who will live as a member of the household for many years, not as simply another Christmas gift," stresses Linda Campbell, director of programs for the Humane Society of Missouri in St. Louis.

Campbell works at the fourth largest shelter in the country. Her shelter stops adopting out dogs between December 15 and January 1 to prevent a high rate of returns in January from people who tried buying dogs for others or who, in their haste, selected the wrong dog for their lifestyle. Her staff also thoroughly interviews all potential adopters to help them make the right match—when the time is right.

If you really want to give a dog as a gift, Campbell recommends a better alternative to adopting a dog during the holidays. Give a gift certificate for a new dog, which can be redeemed after the holidays when schedules are back to normal. If your children are clamoring for a new puppy, wrap all the puppy supplies in decorative paper and bows and let them open these gifts at Christmas. Then begin your search for a puppy after the holidays. Go as a family and select a few finalists before deciding on a dog to adopt. "Selecting a new puppy or a dog needs to be a family decision," says Campbell. "Take your time, look carefully, and pick a dog who meets your family's lifestyle."

there are a lot of options worth considering. If your commute isn't too long, consider going home at the regular time, spending some quality time with your dog, and then continuing with your plans. There's a very good chance that you'll be in a better mood and more productive after discussing your day with your dog and taking the opportunity to unwind. Perhaps you can take work home with you. If those options are not possible, pick up the telephone and have a friend stop by your home at your regular arrival time to give your dog a social thrill. It doesn't take much. An hourlong visit would be great, but any time he or she spends with your dog will do wonders for relieving her stress and your guilt.

Your dog is a creature of habit who gladly lives according to whatever schedule you dictate. If you work nights, your dog will accommodate without complaint. If you work from home, your dog will not only be ecstatic but also will help you constructively use your break times. Some well-trained dogs are even showing up in the workplace—paws up!

If you are going to change schedules abruptly, or periodically, you must allow your dog the opportunity to adjust, or else you'll face the possible consequences.

Don't bother explaining the situation to your dog. You needn't bring home a note from your boss or try to bribe your dog into accepting the situation with a special treat. Concentrate instead on making the change as gradual as possible and allowing your dog to accommodate in the best way possible. The good news is that your dog will never question the reasons for the change but will concentrate instead on making changes in her schedule to match yours. How many people can say that about a significant other?

So should you feel guilty about working, having a social life, and not spending every waking moment with your dog? Absolutely not! As you'll see in coming chapters, you can be a great on-the-go dog owner

If you are running late at work, have a friend stop by to give your dogs a social thrill.

and cause your dog few disappointments. Just respect the fact that your dog is doing everything in her power to meet your needs, and the rest is pretty simple. We'll help guide you through the process!

The very first thing you need to do is establish a schedule that you can live with, and be prepared to stick to it for the sake of your dog. The most important things on the schedule are times when human contact is available and when there is access to food and toilet breaks. We already mentioned that if you (or a substitute) come and go at the same times during the day, you would cause your dog much less anxiety than she'd have not knowing when to expect food or a potty break. You can also appreciate that knowing when you are likely to be fed and get to go to the bathroom would be important considerations for you if you were ever reincarnated as a dog. These are basic needs to be respected and really shouldn't be major impediments to having an on-the-go lifestyle.

If your dog must spend too much time alone, be fair and consider doggy day care centers, pet sitters, or dog walkers to help pass the time. If you really want to be away from home for extended periods and don't want to be concerned with professional pet services, carefully consider your original reasons for wanting a dog.

If you realize that you've made a mistake and really cannot care for your dog properly, follow the guidelines in Chapter 11 to responsibly find your canine companion a new loving home. If you've now realized that owning a dog is the easiest relationship you've ever had to manage, read on! There's a lot of fun ahead.

CHAPTER 2

WAYS TO MAKE YOUR DOG FEEL RIGHT AT HOME

Your dog spends more time inside your home than you do. Let's face it. We need to earn a living to pay off mortgages, car loans, and to buy dog food. We need to drop kids off at school, practice, and other events. We need to go grocery shopping, to doctor appointments, to visit family out of town, to go out with friends. You get the picture. For most of us, that means being eight or more hours away from home at least five days a week.

Yet as you rush to get ready for each new workday or school day, you catch sight of your dog's irresistible pair of sad brown eyes and feel the guilt rising inside you. You hate to leave your canine chum home alone. Playing hooky and spending the day with your dog sounds much more appealing than working on that annual report or attending yet another lecture or company meeting. But let's face it; nobody is going to pay you to stay home with your pooch, so we must deal with reality.

You can free yourself from guilt-ridden thoughts by designing your home with your dog in mind. Most of our tips are free or inexpensive. We'll deal with strategies for making your relationship with your pet rewarding in other chapters; here we just want to concentrate on the physical home environment.

Let's liken the situation to another potentially stressful event. After dating that special someone for a period, you decide the next step should be living together or marriage. Inviting someone into your personal space is stressful, whether it is a significant other or a dog. With your dog, you may not have to worry about freeing up closet space or hiding things that you wouldn't want the other person to discover, but there are considerations. A dog doesn't realize that the dining room table, the leg of which he's using as a chew toy, was given to you by your grandmother and possesses major sentimental value. He also doesn't realize that you didn't mean to share those $300 leather shoes with him, even though you left them in plain view. He just misses you.

Your dog doesn't know he isn't supposed to chew on certain things.

So in this chapter, we're going to help make Peppy feel at home in your space. It's never too early to be thinking long-term, once you start living together. Let's start by taking a room-by-room inspection of your current layout, keeping your dog's needs and wants in mind. Put yourself in your dog's place and ask yourself: *Is this safe? Is this an interesting environment in which to spend the day alone?* Or, if you were in the same situation, would you be looking around for a pair of shoes to chew on, too? While it's best to start preparing your home before you bring a dog into it, you will still find this information worth heeding if you already have a special canine someone living with you. You can relax knowing as you head out the door for work that your home-alone dog will be content.

Cater to Your Canine's Creature Comforts

While you're away, your dog spends most of his time snoozing. But during his waking time, he needs items to activate his play mode as well as to help him engage in activities that make him feel safe and comfortable. If he doesn't have appropriate items of his own to keep him entertained, you can bet that he'll be looking at your possessions to meet those needs.

One of the first issues to address is whether you will give your new four-legged roommate access to your entire dwelling or only parts of it. If there are certain places that are definitely off-limits to your new friend, make it clear from the start by always

Your dog needs appropriate items of his own to keep him entertained.

closing doors or setting up child safety gates as barriers. As the years go on and you and your friend better understand each other's rules, barriers become less important. But don't underestimate their importance in the beginning. If it took you four days to compose a business proposal in your home office and you come home one day to find your pooch batting it around the living room and shredding it into confetti, realize that it was your fault for not blocking his access to that area of your home when unsupervised. Don't blame your dog for not understanding how important the document was to you and your career.

Furniture is an issue that you might as well deal with from the start as well. If you have expensive furniture and you like to entertain at home, realize that your dog will want to share the furniture that you use. That doesn't mean that your furniture will become a furry mess. If your dog has full run of the house, the best option is to buy an inexpensive couch or easy chair that is fine for

How to Make Your Home Your Dog's Castle

✔ Open the window blinds to allow warm sunshine to pour in and to give your dog a good perch that allows him to release his curiosity and keep tabs on what's going on in his neighborhood.

✔ Have tile or hardwood floors? Strategically locate some comfy rugs, large pillows, or a doggy bed to cushion these hard surfaces for your dog's siestas. Place these body comforters in warm, cozy places out of drafts, especially if you have an old dog or one with arthritis.

✔ Introduce your dog to the canine version of a scavenger hunt. Hide healthy treats in different places in your house before you leave for work in the morning. The hours will fly by when your dog hunts down these tasty treats. Ditto for his favorite toys. When you arrive home, praise him for the booty he has found.

✔ Leave the radio on and tuned in to your dog's favorite music. Some dogs dig jazz; others like classical or rock. Some like talk radio and get comfort from hearing human voices. You could also set your television on a timer so that it turns on and off—maybe tune it into a twenty-four-hour animal cable station. These sounds and sights from the radio and television help take away some feeling of loneliness in your dog.

✔ Stock your home with durable toys that pass the chew test. Give your dog hard rubber, latex, or nylon toys. Don't buy toys made of soft foam or other material that can easily be shred into small pieces and cause accidental choking. Also, do not give your dog your old shoes or clothing to play with. He may have problems distinguishing why old tennis shoes are an acceptable chew but not the expensive pumps in your closet.

✔ Stuff a hard rubber ball or toy such as a Kong toy with your dog's favorite food treat. Topping the list of food favorites for most dogs are peanut butter, cheese, meat, or kibble. While you're gone, your dog will spend hours trying to retrieve every last morsel from these food-dispensing toys. New varieties of this food-in-a-ball concept are battery operated and allow you to leave personal messages up to 15 seconds long. Each time your dog noses the ball and makes it move, your voice is activated. You could leave a message such as, "Good boy, Sam. That's right. Nudge the ball and you'll get a tasty treat. You can do it!" These food-dispensing activities also help save wear and tear on your furniture caused by a bored or anxious dog.

✔ Call your dog one or two times a day from work. Leave a friendly message on the answering machine such as, "Hey, Rocky, how's it going, boy? Daddy will be home in a few hours and will take you on a nice long walk." To save your dignity, select a time when you can make a private call, and deny ever doing this to others, especially coworkers who don't own pets and won't understand your friendship bond.

✔ Consider installing a doggy door. More on this later, but a doggy door permits your well-behaved dog to get some fresh air and relieve himself, even when you are not around.

Your dog will want to share the furniture that you use. One option is to buy an inexpensive couch that you both can enjoy.

your dog to use. Both of you should use it together regularly—for cuddling, watching television, or just discussing the day's events. Save the good furniture for when you are entertaining, and move the pet-friendly furniture to another room. When you are at work, your friend will naturally gravitate to the furniture that you share; the expensive furniture will have little or no appeal. Hopefully.

If that fails, go with Plan B. Cover your expensive furniture with sheets when you go out, realiz-

ing that they become your pet's furniture once you leave and the door is closed. When you come home, simply remove the sheet, fold it, and tuck it out of sight behind the couch, especially when you are expecting company. The sheet on the sofa could hamper impromptu get-togethers when you want to invite people back to your home, unless your guests are as pet loving as you are. Consistency is key. You have to be diligent to always remember to put the sheets on the furniture or be prepared to live with the hairy consequences.

Meet the McGoverns

As president of PetsMart.com, Tom McGovern is top dog at the on-line company, but he and his wife, Tammy, readily admit that their three-bedroom home is ruled by a pair of rescued dogs named Norris and Millie. And both dogs are intentionally spoiled. "We love our dogs and want them to feel like members of our family," says McGovern.

A tour through their home quickly indicates how the McGoverns have made their home fit for their dogs. Toys of all shapes are scattered throughout the living room. Nap-inviting doggy beds are strategically placed in various rooms. A doggy door opens to a fenced backyard, where the focal point isn't a gas grill or a lavish landscape but a pair of cool-looking doggy igloos with bottomless bowls of water out front. "Millie and Norris have access to every possible new toy that comes out in the market," he says. "In a way, they act as my product testers."

Multiply the Meals at Chow Time

Despite what you may have heard rumored in doggy circles, it is actually better to feed your dog two or three small meals during the day rather than one large meal. At the very least, plan on feeding your dog twice a day, once at breakfast time and once at supper time. If you have a miniature or toy breed, even twice-daily feedings might not be enough to fend off bouts of hypoglycemia (seriously). Fear not! There are alternative ways to feed your pet at regular hours, even when you are not there to do it yourself.

Dewclaws up to technology! Thanks to some ingenious inventors, you no longer have to worry about whether your dog has fresh water and food if you need to be gone for longer than expected. This can come in handy if that certain someone invites you out to dinner or drinks after work and you don't want to decline with the excuse that you have to go home to feed your dog.

Consider buying food-dispensing devices that can hold up to a seven-day supply of dry food as well as timer-controlled food dispensers that release a preset amount of food. If 5:00 P.M. rolls around and you're not home, your dog still gets his meal right on time. You're able to determine the portion size, so the dispenser doesn't turn into an all-you-can-eat smorgasbord for your food-happy hound, and, with a week's supply, you save time each day on feeding your dog. There are also canine drinking fountains that circulate and filter your dog's drinking water, which keep the water tasting fresh when you're not there to change it.

These devices can also prove to be life savers for your pet in the event that you are unexpectedly unable to return home for a couple of days, perhaps due to a natural disaster or other type of emergency. Available supplies of food and water can prevent your pet from starving to death or becoming dehydrated.

It is better to feed your dog two or three small meals a day rather than one large meal.

To make dinnertime even more special, raise your dog's food and water bowls by buying an elevated bowl holder or placing the bowls on a sturdy child's step stool or wooden platform. Adjust the height to meet your dog's size. This simple technique helps relieve neck and back strain in your dog, and might also help prevent problems in dogs prone to bloat. It's a simple but caring way to make dogs with special needs feel a bit more comfortable while they nibble away at food.

Bathroom Solutions for the Housebound Dog

Just thinking about being denied a bathroom for eight or more hours is enough to make us cross our legs in panic. Yet somehow we expect that of our indoor dogs. In this day of dual-income families and congested highways, we can't always get home as early as intended.

Keeping your dog outdoors with a fenced yard and a doghouse or a dog run works great in mild climates, but what about dogs living in the snowbelt states or in high-rise apartments? Fortunately, relief has arrived to keep your home accident-free and your dog's bladder from working overtime. Among new options that beat lining your home with newspapers are doggy litter boxes, portable toilets, and asking a neighbor kid to walk your dog.

Potty Solutions

✔ **Doggy Litter Boxes:** Why should cats monopolize this market? The day of indoor bathrooms for dogs has arrived. Specially designed doggy litter boxes are ideal when you are house-training a puppy or need to provide a suitable indoor outlet for a senior dog with a weak bladder. The litter is made of highly absorbent recycled paper and wood pulp products. Just scoop up the deposits daily. Doggy litter and boxes (available in various sizes) are available at most pet supply stores. You'll need to provide positive words of encouragement to entice your dog to use the litter box, and always praise and reward him for a job well done.

✔ **Portable Toilet:** Inventor Joni MacLaine is a stand-up comedian who found it was no laughing matter that her aging Pekingese, Sugar, could no longer control her bladder all day. MacLaine came up with a clever solution. She created a portable doggy potty that can be placed anywhere inside the house (or on the balcony for folks living in high-rise apartments). Called the Patio Park, this doggy toilet consists of a 2-by-4-foot piece of real grass, a water reservoir, a mock fire hydrant, liner bags, an irrigation system, and a 22-inch-high plastic splash guard that is easy to clean. The self-irrigating device assembles in a matter of minutes, and you need to replace the sod only once a month. Your dogs get the sense of the real outdoors, and you don't have to deal with any foul odor.

✔ **Rent-a-Kid:** Sometimes the easiest solution is to have a friend or neighbor kid come to your home to give your dog a toilet break in the middle of the day and hopefully to play a little as well. What a great tension reliever to have a friend come by to play!

Ask a neighbor kid to come and give your dog a potty break.

You may not want to discuss your dog's toilet habits in polite company, but we count on impeccable house-training when we bring dogs into our homes. Don't make the process harder than it needs to be. We'll be discussing proper house-breaking, or house-training, in another chapter. For now, it is just important to realize that successful house-training requires that your dog have every opportunity to succeed, and that means being given the opportunity to relieve himself in a suitable location when the need arises (not when it is convenient for you). Dogs can hold it for a long time once properly trained, but don't test the limits. How would you feel under the same circumstances?

Play It Safe

Without even realizing it, dogs have a way of making us all better housekeepers. While dogs aren't as curious as cats are, they can get into a heap of trouble when left home alone. Whenever possible, create no-pet zones by simply shutting the doors to certain rooms or installing doorway barriers with safety latches designed for toddlers. But that's not always possible or practical. Even some stubby-legged dachshunds can prove to be better leapers than anticipated. If your dog is a climber, consider metal doggy gates that are vertical in length without any horizontal bars in the middle to provide them an easy boost to go up and over the gate. You need to size up the total height of the gate to make sure it is long enough to stop a leaper.

The smell of food is hard for your dog to resist. Installing doorway barriers designed for toddlers will help keep him out of trouble.

The smell of food scraps in the kitchen garbage can be too much of a temptation for any dog to resist. Or he may try to fend off boredom by grabbing the end of your new roll of toilet paper and strewing tissue banners down your hallway. The solution is to think of your dog as a toddler and childproof/dog proof your home.

In every room, make sure that all electrical cords are out of reach. We recommend using safety electrical cords and ground fault interrupted

(GFI) circuits that prevent shocks or sparks if chewed on. Break your dog of this bad habit by dusting the cords with Bitter Apple spray or cayenne pepper. Most dogs don't like the taste of these substances, but some dogs eventually develop an acquired taste for them. Also consider securing loose cords to the floor or baseboards

Make sure you don't leave any toxic plants within your dogs reach.

(just be careful not to insert a tack or staple directly into the cord wire).

Protect your dog from falls. Always keep lower windows shut and locked to keep your dog in and burglars out. High-rise syndrome is the undesirable end result when a pet falls from an apartment window or balcony. If you live in a high-rise or have a balcony, be aware that pets can fall from balconies. Make sure that never happens by attaching sheets of hard plastic or chicken wire (available at hardware stores) to your balcony railing to prevent your pet from slipping through or under the railing.

If you love indoor plants, hang them on ceiling hooks, out of your dog's reach. Skip these common varieties, which can be potentially lethal if eaten by your dog:

- ✔ Aloe vera
- ✔ Amaryllis
- ✔ Azalea
- ✔ Creeping fig
- ✔ Daffodil
- ✔ Dieffenbachia
- ✔ Elephant's ear
- ✔ Geraniums
- ✔ Holly
- ✔ Impatiens
- ✔ Ivy
- ✔ Mistletoe
- ✔ Morning glory
- ✔ Oleander
- ✔ Philodendron
- ✔ Poinsettia (gets a lot of press, but it isn't likely as toxic as initially believed)
- ✔ Spider chrysanthemum
- ✔ Yew

Unsure if one of your plants is toxic? Check with the HSUS. The HSUS Web site (www.hsus.org) provides a complete list of dangerous plants.

If you still enjoy plants, opt for these safe types inside your home:

- ✔ African violet
- ✔ Baby rubber plant
- ✔ Boston fern
- ✔ Coleus
- ✔ Hibiscus
- ✔ Hoya
- ✔ Jade plant
- ✔ Schefflera
- ✔ Spider plant
- ✔ Zebra plant

Do a Room-By-Room Assessment

Let's start in the kitchen. Stash kitchen garbage in heavy-lidded containers (which also control odors) or, better yet, inside a latched cabinet. We recommend placing inexpensive (and easy-to-install) plastic childproof latches on every cabinet door within paw's reach. Even if you own a Houdini hound, these latches will protect your dog from rifling through the trash can and choking on a chicken bone or cutting his mouth on a discarded metal can lid.

Check out the kitchen counters and the dining room table. Clear them of any food temptations your dog can nose out; ditto for sharp utensils or breakable glass items. All it takes is a rigorous tail wag or an accidental thump into the side of a table for a steak knife or wineglass to tumble onto the ground. If you don't have time to do the dishes, store them in the sink or dishwasher. Make sure that the coffee maker and other appliances are back on the counter against the wall and well out of paw's reach.

Let's move into your living room. Survey the scene as if you were an excitable Labrador retriever—not a home decorator for the rich and famous. You can still show off your decorative style simply by doing a little rearranging. Relocate antique vases and other breakables to safe places out of the path of a dodging, darting dog. Those items can be placed inside an enclosed display cabinet (less dusting for you!) or perched high up on a sturdy bookcase. Don't forget your television remote control and other objects that your dog can easily grab in his mouth. Keep them off low-level coffee tables and tuck them inside a drawer or place them on top of your television set before you head out the door.

Now for the bedrooms. Keep loose coins in narrow-necked capped bottles. Store earrings, rings, cuff links, and necklaces in fastened jewelry boxes or inside nightstand drawers. Some dogs can't resist these shiny metal objects and end up swallowing them and possibly choking on them. Stash shoes and other tempting chewables inside closed closet doors. By getting into the habit of storing these items, you will benefit by knowing where they are (a real time-saver, especially on those workday mornings). Plus, by closing your closet doors, you make your bedroom appear less cluttered.

Finish with the bathrooms. Install childproof latches on the cabinets. When you're gone, make bathrooms off-limits by keeping doors shut. But if you forget to close the door, that's where those cabinet latches come in handy. The poisonous chemicals inside the house-cleaning products are safe inside these protected cabinets. Even better, store these hazardous items in a high cabinet far out of paw's reach. Don't assume that these chemicals are so caustic that your dog would have no interest in consuming them. Officials at the ASPCA/National Animal Poison Control Center are constantly educating pet owners about these household dangers and others. Don't forget about those shampoos, razors, and other items in your bathtub. We recommend storing them on racks out

Positive Crate-Training

If you want to confine your puppy or dog to one area of the house or apartment, consider an indoor exercise pen or a dog crate. These plastic or wire kennels come in a variety of sizes and give your home-alone dog a lot of safe space. Place his bed and food at one end, and, if necessary, place newspaper on the opposite end to act as an emergency bathroom. Dogs prize cleanliness and don't want to spoil their sleeping quarters.

Crates are great when used properly. Dogs are den animals by nature. They like to nestle and rest inside cozy protective environments. The problem arises when crates are misused and confine dogs for extended periods of time. Crates should be safe retreats, not prison cells for dogs. Your dog needs to associate the crate with positive praise from you and quiet solace. Never stick your dog inside a crate as a punishment for misbehaving. You will only end up confusing your dog about the role the crate serves.

To make the crate rank as one of your dog's favorite places, follow these steps:

1. Assemble the crate and put it in a busy area of the house, such as the kitchen, so your dog will not feel abandoned or isolated.
2. Leave the door open. Cover the flooring with comfy bedding, and place one of your dog's favorite toys inside.
3. When your curious dog checks out the crate, tell him, "Go to your crate," and toss a tasty treat inside.
4. Keep the door open so that your dog can enter and leave at will to build up his trust of the crate.
5. Once your dog displays confidence in entering the crate, try feeding him an occasional meal inside the crate, placing his food bowl in the back end.
6. Toss one of his toys into the crate. As he plays with it, close the crate door without a lot of fanfare. Keep the door closed for a few minutes and praise your dog.
7. Extend the length of time you keep your dog inside the crate. Your dog will soon learn that the crate represents a great place to get treats and catch some afternoon naps without being disturbed.

of paw's reach. Place them on a lightweight multi-tiered shelf that can hang from your showerhead or a high window ledge, or attach to the wall inside your shower or tub.

Get everyone in the household to practice toilet safety tactics. Keep a lid on the situation at all times, literally, by always keeping the toilet lid down. Your dog doesn't need to be drinking the germ-filled bowl water. If your dog loves to unroll the toilet paper, fasten a rubber band around it or install an inexpensive toilet paper cover to keep your dog from pawing at the paper.

Don't Forget the Garage

Your dog should spend only minimal time in the garage, and only when you're around to supervise. There are too many dangers inside a garage, ranging from tools and power equipment to antifreeze puddles on the floor. Most antifreeze contains ethylene glycol (EG), a sweet-tasting but potentially deadly substance to dogs. In some cases, all it takes is 2 ounces to kill a dog. The chemical, once ingested, crystallizes and attacks and destroys your dog's kidneys, the filtering organs. Consider switching to pet-friendly antifreeze that contains propylene glycol (PG). This new type of antifreeze works just as well as the traditional EG types but isn't toxic to pets. And, because it doesn't contain phosphates, this biodegradable antifreeze is also environmentally friendly.

Not many of us keep tidy garages. There are also potential hazards on the floor, such as old nails that could puncture your dog's footpad or an opened bag of fertilizer that could be ingested and cause abdominal problems in your too-curious canine.

Finally, most garages are poorly ventilated. A dog housed inside your garage while you're gone could become overheated during hot months or overly chilled during cold months.

Open the Way to the Great Outdoors

As a full-fledged member of your family, your dog should spend most of his days and all of his nights inside your home. If you're fortunate to have a fenced backyard, we recommend installing a doggy door to allow your well-behaved dog free access to indoors and outdoors while you're away. A doggy door allows your dog to check out what's happening outside—safely. And it melts away your worries about racing home in time to let your dog out to go potty.

Select a doggy door that best meets your type of home construction. Various models can be installed in existing doors or walls, or set up as separate panels that act as extensions to sliding glass doors. These come in handy if you rent instead of own your home because you won't be making major

---

Bow-"Ow" Medical Kits

You come home and find bloody paw prints all over the floor. You may not be able to prevent every accident, but you can be prepared. That's why your home should have a dog first aid kit that can treat minor mishaps. Keep this kit in the same place you store your first aid kit. In fact, if you have a first aid kit for yourself, it's probably fine for your dog as well, but we recommend you have a separate rectal thermometer just for your dog. Some things are better not shared. There are commercial dog kits available from pet supply stores, mail catalogs, and on-line Web sites. Or make your own by stocking it with these items:

- Antibiotic ointment
- Antiseptic wipes
- Benadryl for insect bites and stings
- Coated buffered aspirin (never give your dog acetaminophen or ibuprofen)
- Cold packs
- Cotton balls
- Cotton-tipped swabs
- Heat packs

- Lightweight adhesive tape that doesn't stick to minor wounds
- Nonstick sterile gauze pads
- Phone numbers of your family veterinarian, an emergency pet clinic, and the ASPCA National Animal Poison Control Center (888-426-4435)
- Rectal thermometer
- Tweezers

changes to the structure of the building. Once your dog is outside, you should designate one special area in which your dog should do his business. With very little training, your dog will go to this one area to relieve himself. This makes cleanup easier and the risk of disease transmission less likely.

Choosing a "Guest House"

If your dog is going to be spending any time outdoors on your property, he deserves his own "guest house." In selecting a doghouse that protects a dog from nasty weather, we make these recommendations:

✓ Choose one that can be made mobile. Attach the doghouse to four wheels so you can relocate it easily without straining your back. You can move it to a shady spot on hot, humid days and to a sunny place in the winter. This also prevents the house from killing the grass beneath it.

✓ Size does matter. Select a model that is wide enough for your dog to turn around in and long enough for him to stretch out without touching the sides or poking out the front door. Resist the temptation of buying a mega-sized house for a mini-sized dog. Dogs depend on their body heat inside confined spaces to keep from shivering on cold days.

✓ Make sure the doghouse is well ventilated and that the entrance is not in the direct path of prevailing winds.

✓ Attach a thick clear plastic flap on the front door to let your dog easily go in and out. The flap keeps out bugs, rain, sleet, and snow, and it provides a clear window for your dog to keep tabs on his surroundings.

✓ Select models with floors that are at least 4 inches off the ground and that have slanted roofs so that snow, ice, and rain won't pile up on top.

✓ Spray the doghouse interior once a week with flea and tick spray.

And always make sure your dog has access to water outdoors. Is your dog a bowl-spiller? Place a large, heavy rock in the center of the bowl to keep it anchored. Better yet, provide a couple of water bowls to ensure an adequate supply. Always provide fresh water daily.

Prepare for the Unexpected Escape

Even though your dog appears safe inside your home, the unexpected could happen. He could pop open a screen window or figure out a way to get over—or under—the fence and be roaming the neighborhood while you're not home. That's why we recommend heeding a lesson from the Boy Scouts: "Be prepared."

You always carry your driver's license, and your dog should always wear some form of identification (ID). An ID tag that contains your contact information on a collar is a good start. For added insurance, consider having your veterinarian surgically implant a microchip ID under your dog's skin. More and more animal shelters and veterinary clinics have the equipment to scan a dog for a microchip ID. If your lost dog has a microchip, the shelter or clinic can contact you. The tag and the microchip help increase the chances of you and your dog being reunited quickly.

CHAPTER 3

* * * * * * * * *

KEEPING AN URBAN/SUBURBAN DOG HEALTHY

* * * * * * * * *

We have practically everything it takes to ensure that our dogs live longer and healthier lives, from designer foods to pacemaker implants. No longer is the visit to a veterinarian's office limited to routine vaccinations and an annual physical examination. Depending on a dog's needs, some veterinary clinics can offer high-tech care with everything from computerized axial tomography (CAT) scans to organ transplant surgery. More and more veterinarians are skilled at performing total hip replacement surgery, allergy tests, root canals, and cataract surgeries. And that's just the beginning. The world of canine health care keeps expanding and improving, with our dogs reaping the benefits.

How to Keep Your Dog Healthy

✔ Select the right veterinarian
✔ Find a substitute caretaker
✔ Keep up on the vaccination schedule
✔ Maintain regular dental care
✔ Select the right dog food
✔ Provide flea and tick protection
✔ Provide senior care
✔ Be prepared for emergencies
✔ Buy pet insurance
✔ Be prepared for disasters

Shopping for a Veterinarian

The very best time to shop for a veterinarian is before you adopt a dog. Yes, use that dogless time to locate a veterinarian who will be able to fit your lifestyle and have the skills to provide lifelong care for your dog. Temporarily focus on you, not your future dog. In shopping for the ideal veterinarian, consider these factors:

● Does your job sometimes require you to work long hours? If you don't get home until after 7:00 P.M., look for a clinic that offers evening and weekend hours.

● If you work various shifts or an odd work schedule, consider walk-in clinics, mobile clinics, or veterinarians who make house calls. They can fit into your schedule.

● What is the medical training of the veterinary staff members? Are they willing to let you take a tour of the facilities? Do they attend training conferences regularly to keep up to date on the latest veterinary medical care?

● Does the veterinarian offer arrangements for after hours or emergency medical care to his or her clients? Is there a brochure or business card readily available at the counter for you to take and keep in an easy-to-reach place in your home?

The bottom line is that as an on-the-go dog owner, you want service when you need service. While you're shopping for the best place, find out the clinic's payment policy and what auxiliary services it provides, such as boarding and grooming. Too often, dog owners select veterinarians based on who happens to be the closest, but you'll save yourself time, money, and anguish if you select one who can accommodate your busy schedule and care for your dog the way you need that care to be delivered.

Locating a Stand-In Caretaker

Next up, find a suitable stand-in who can care for your dog in case you aren't available, whether you're on a planned trip or you have to take off on a moment's notice. Locate someone you trust who can step in and care for your dog during your absence. That person can be a family member, a friend, or a professional pet sitter. Whomever you pick, provide the person with the contact information for your veterinary clinic. Also make arrangements in advance with your veterinarian to pay for medical care for your dog in your absence. Even though many veterinary clinics post the sign, "Payment due when services are rendered," you can make prior arrangements with your veterinarian. One solution is to provide written authorization to the veterinary clinic to permit your dog's caretaker to use your credit card if your dog should get sick and need medical attention when you're not available. If you have insurance for your canine dependent (and you should), there will be a lot fewer expenses that end up on that credit card than might otherwise be the case.

The best time to shop for a veterinarian is before you adopt a dog.

For the busy pet owner, there are even payment cards that can be used specifically for veterinary care. These are extremely handy to leave with canine caregivers. These credit cards can be used only in veterinary hospitals, so you don't have to worry about a caregiver using your card for unauthorized purchases at the local shopping mall.

Vaccines

There's plenty of controversy and uncertainty regarding vaccinations, but don't consider it an option in the care of your dog. With vaccines, it's all about protection. You never want to be the one who brought parvo (parvovirus) to the party. And in this mobile society, you want to help your dog avoid certain regional medical maladies such as Lyme disease, which is common in the wooded areas of the Northeast (as well as in other areas).

Certain vaccinations are mandatory, and they protect your canine pal against many infectious diseases. Just as kids need certain vaccinations to be allowed into schools, dogs need them to get into boarding facilities, to stay at a hospital veterinary clinic, and to cross the

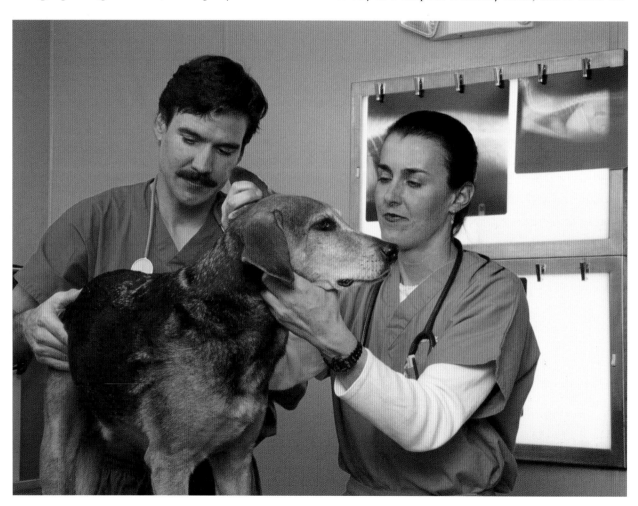

Although only certain vaccinations are mandatory, there are other "must have" vaccinations that your veterinarian will recommend.

border or get on a plane. In short, vaccines are designed to keep your dog healthy in all types of social settings.

Topping the list is the rabies vaccination, mainly required as a public health measure. The vaccine is usually first given at 12 weeks of age, followed by a booster one year later and then once every one to three years, depending on where you live and the regional risk of infection. It protects your dog against this viral disease that attacks the nervous system and is often spread by saliva, usually from animal bites. It is important to realize that the rabies vaccination, while important for dogs, is actually mandated for our protection. Vaccinated dogs and cats serve as a useful buffer between people and rabies in other species. Thus, in countries that regularly vaccinate dogs, such as the United States and Canada, most rabies cases are seen in wildlife and livestock. In Mexico, where vaccination of dogs and cats is not as routine, dogs are the most common carriers of rabies.

Other "Must" Vaccines Protect Dogs Against:

✔ **Parvovirus:** A viral disease that causes severe vomiting, bloody diarrhea, and dehydration

✔ **Distemper:** A contagious viral disease that causes fever, appetite loss, pneumonia, and, in severe cases, encephalitis, convulsive seizures, paralysis, and even death

✔ **Hepatitis:** An infectious disease (known medically as adenovirus) that causes stomach pain, vomiting or diarrhea, liver swelling, and inflammation of the eyes

Keeping your dog vaccinated is the best thing you can do to keep yourself protected from rabies.

Many veterinarians recommend that you vaccinate your dog against coronavirus and parainfluenza. Coronavirus causes all the same clinical signs (symptoms) as parvovirus, but they are usually less severe. Parainfluenza is one of the viral causes of canine cough, an extremely contagious respiratory disease of dogs that is frequently complicated by bacterial infections. Depending on what part of the country you live in or where you might be vacationing with your dog, Lyme disease and leptospirosis vaccines may also be needed.

If you're going to board your dog or keep her in close confines with other dogs, it's a good idea to have your dog vaccinated for canine cough with a *Bordetella* vaccination, in addition to the parainfluenza inoculation. As mentioned previously, canine cough is a contagious respiratory infection characterized by a hacking cough that can persist for weeks. Even though the vaccine (which, by the way, is squirted up your dog's nose, not injected) does not guarantee that your dog won't pick up a version of canine cough, it offers some preventive protection.

Discuss with your veterinarian the vaccination schedule best suited for your dog's needs in your local area. Just realize that growing puppies must get a series of vaccinations between the ages of six weeks and four months. After that, all dogs typically should get booster vaccinations at one year of age and then regularly thereafter.

Dental Care

When it comes to your dog, be down in her mouth—literally. You should make weekly inspections of your dog's teeth and gums so that you can correct a problem before it escalates into an expensive one.

Learn how to brush your dog's teeth with some regularity. Our ancestors didn't brush their teeth, and this very likely had a direct impact on their longevity. The same holds true for dogs. When dogs had a life span of only 5 to 8 years, they had their teeth for a lifetime, even if those teeth weren't very healthy by the end. Now, however, with superior veterinary care, great nutrition, and parasite control, dogs are living an average of 12 to 14 years. They need a healthy set of choppers to serve them through their golden years.

You probably hoped that biscuit treats and chew toys would provide the dental cleaning your dog needs, but they only help; they do not do the whole job. These products work by their abrasive action on the tooth surface. But if you own a hungry hound who inhales her treats, chances are slim to none that any of these teeth-cleaning benefits occurred. Since most plaque and tartar accumulates on and under the gum line and not on the chewing surface of the teeth, treats and chew toys never get the whole job done. Just like people, dogs develop a plaque film on their teeth after meals. If it is not regularly removed, the plaque becomes calcified into tartar, that hard brown crud that appears on your dog's teeth. Doggy breath develops when the teeth are not clean or when plaque accumulates under the gum line. Yuck!

So invest in a canine toothbrush and some doggy dentifrice (toothpaste) and get to work. If you're having trouble, get your veterinarian to show you how it is done. Be patient and thorough, and your dog will own a winning smile for her lifetime.

Have your veterinarian perform a regular dental examination as part of your dog's routine physical evaluation. Be prepared that at some point, even if you religiously brush your dog's teeth, your dog will require a professional dental cleaning under the

---

Helpful Tips on Brushing Your Dog's Teeth

- ✔ Introduce teeth brushing to your dog when she's a puppy so that she gets used to it.
- ✔ Gradually introduce teeth brushing to your older dog.
- ✔ Make teeth brushing fun. Speak in an upbeat manner and give plenty of praise during the brushing and a treat after brushing.
- ✔ Keep brushing sessions to a few minutes at a time. Heap on plenty of praise to encourage your dog.
- ✔ Start by dipping a finger into beef bouillon and rub your flavored finger across your dog's gums and teeth.
- ✔ Then introduce gauze over your finger and gently scrub your dog's teeth in a circular motion.
- ✔ Finally, introduce a soft doggy toothbrush and use a flavored toothpaste made especially for dogs.

gum line to prevent or treat gingivitis. This is a common procedure and often referred to as a "prophy." It does not mean that you have been doing a bad job. Your dentist or dental hygienist does something similar for you at your regular cleanings, and this helps clear bacteria out of pockets that can develop under the gums. With proper dental hygiene, there is no reason your dog should not have fresh breath.

Nutrition

This isn't a book about nutrition, so you won't get a lecture about food groups and portion sizes, but your dog is what she eats. Dogs don't sneak out at midnight and gobble down a couple of burgers and a shake on their own. They rely on you to provide them with meals.

Feeding a dog can be an awesome responsibility. Whether you are trying to impose a vegetarian lifestyle on your dog, want to buy the cheapest food available (or the most expensive), or feel the need to supplement with vitamins, minerals, oils, or herbs, don't make uninformed decisions. First discuss dietary needs for your dog with your veterinarian.

Fortunately, there are plenty of nutritious commercial dog foods available. The challenge, however, comes in choosing the right food to suit the age, health, and level of activity of your dog. What may be ideal for your neighbor's laid-back 10-year-old basset hound may be totally wrong for your hyper 2-year-old Jack Russell terrier.

It is important to discuss your dog's dietary needs with your veterinarian.

As for price, the cheapest dog foods tend to contain the highest levels of fiber. The most expensive diets usually pack the highest levels of protein. Chances are that neither extreme is best for your dog. For an average dog who gets an average amount of exercise, dog foods in the middle price bracket are usually the best bets.

Like human diets, most commercial canine diets provide way more calories than required to meet nutritional needs. Accordingly, obesity is about as common in dogs as it is in people. In fact, obesity is

Nutritional Facts and Get-Fit Tips

✔ **Caloric intake:** A 10-pound dog, on average, needs between 400 and 500 calories of food a day to maintain a healthy weight. A 20-pound dog needs 700 to 800 calories, and a 75-pound dog needs between 1,750 and 2,000 calories per day.

✔ **Watch out for hidden calories:** One teaspoon of vegetable oil added to dry food equals 50 calories. For a little dog who needs only 300 calories per day, that one teaspoon can make a big difference in gaining or losing weight.

✔ If your dog has suddenly lost or gained weight, book an appointment with your veterinarian to have your dog examined for any possible medical conditions.

✔ Feed your dog two or three small meals per day, not one large one. (The act of eating burns 10 to 15 percent of ingested calories.)

✔ Measure your dog's food; don't guess the amount. The extra amounts add up to added pounds.

✔ Weigh your dog weekly and note any gains. Keep in mind that 5 extra pounds on a dog who should weigh 17 pounds equates to 50 extra pounds on a person who should weigh 170 pounds.

✔ Keep a food diary and write down everything you feed your dog in a week. You may be surprised by the amount and types of foods you feed him.

✔ Switch from table scraps to healthier snacks such as raw carrots, raw cauliflower, air-popped popcorn, and ice cubes. Or set aside one-third of your dog's daily kibble and offer the food as treats for good behavior throughout the day. Store this kibble in your dog's treat jar.

✔ Work with your veterinarian to cut back the calories gradually and steadily. A dog who is 30 percent overweight should take six months to reach her ideal weight through reduced portions.

✔ Avoid drastic weight-loss plans. Yo-yo dieting (losing and gaining quickly) can cause loss of muscle mass besides fat loss.

✔ Decrease the amount of food offered as your dog ages. Older dogs tend to burn two to four times fewer calories than young dogs do.

the most common nutritional ill among dogs, with one out of every three dogs in this country packing excess pounds.

Finally, a nutritious diet can actually add years to your dog's life. Like you, your dog needs a balanced diet containing all the essential nutrients in the right proportions to keep her immune system strong, her organs in top working shape, and her bones and muscles healthy and toned.

Parasites

Making fleas flee and ticks vamoose has never been easier or safer for the whole family, thanks to the sophisticated chemical warfare being used on these pesky pests. With the creation of safe pills and liquid drops, there should be no need for messy flea powders, marginally effective flea collars, and the dreaded flea bombs. Organophosphates, organochlorines, and carbamates need never be

Flea and Tick Tips

In selecting a flea/tick product, consult with your veterinarian and keep these points in mind:

✔ **Age and status of your dog.** Some products are not recommended for puppies or pregnant or nursing dogs.

✔ **Degree of flea infestation in your home.** Some products are more preventive; others kill adult fleas only.

✔ **Your geography.** If your area is prone to ticks or heartworm, you should consider flea products that also work on these other parasites.

✔ **Household budget.** Most monthly flea products require a veterinarian's prescription that must be factored into your household budget.

✔ **The type of pets in your household.** Some flea and tick products work effectively on dogs and cats; others are strictly designed for dogs and may be toxic to cats. If you also have a cat in your home, don't use a cat-toxic product on your dog.

part of your vocabulary. *Safe* and *effective* are the watchwords these days for flea and tick control.

The flea/tick revolution kicked into high gear in the early 1990s when strong, smart, and safe chemical products became available through veterinarians. Many of these products require only once-a-month application. You can still find harsh insecticides in over-the-counter preparations, but why would you use them?

Arm yourself with knowledge. Even if chemistry wasn't your favorite subject in school, it's helpful to understand how each flea-fighting and tick-tussling chemical works.

Insect growth regulators (IGRs) were the first major development in smart flea control. They don't actually kill fleas—they just stop the immature forms from ever developing into adults, which are the forms that do the biting. In this regard, they work sort of like birth control devices for fleas. Dogs, people, cats, and other mammals lack the flea hormone on which the IGR acts, which makes these products extremely safe for all of us. Products that fit this description include pyriproxyfen, methoprene, and fenoxycarb. A related compound lufenuron (Program) is more correctly termed an insect development inhibitor. Once again, it doesn't kill fleas, but it does stop any fleas that ever bite a dog from producing eggs that will hatch.

Once-a-month remedies seem to have caught on—perhaps it's just convenient, but the trend has spread to some new insecticides as well. You're probably tired of hearing chemical names, but it's very cool if you can rattle some of them off in your veterinarian's office. Some of the better-known once-a-month topical compounds include selamectin (Revolution), fipronil (Frontline), and imidacloprid (Advantage). Many of these products, either alone or in combination, also control other parasites such as ticks, ear mites, and even sarcoptic mange. If you have specific needs, discuss these with your veterinarian. These new wonder products have dramatic effects on fleas, but it may take twenty-four hours for that full effect to be realized. Not to worry. For those who need to hit fleas hard and see the effects in a shorter time, an oral product, nitenpyram (Capstar), kills 98 to 100 percent of fleas on a dog within three to four hours! Nitenpyram should be used on an as-needed basis for flea infestation, but it doesn't pack the 30-day residual control of the other preparations.

So whether you're looking for a full month of flea control, fast flea death, flea control without actually killing fleas, an oral preparation, or a dab-on medication, there's something at your veterinarian's office that's just right for you. Be environmentally conscious, and don't use products that poison you and your pets while attempting to get rid of fleas.

And you no longer need to be ticked off by the presence of ticks on your dog. Ticks, all by themselves, are disgusting, but even more alarming are the diseases that they transmit. You've probably heard of Lyme disease, but there are a host of others that can affect you as well as your dog, including ehrlichiosis (tick fever), Rocky Mountain spotted fever, and babesiosis. It's easy to see ticks on your own skin, but it is more of a challenge when your furry companion is affected.

Whenever you and your dog have taken a stroll in a tick-infested area (especially in forests, grassy or wooded areas, or parks), be prepared to do a head-to-tail inspection afterward to search for ticks. They can be tricky, so make sure you spend time looking in the ears, between the toes, and everywhere else. Ticks need to be attached twenty-four to seventy-two hours before they transmit most of the yucky diseases we alluded to earlier, so you do have a window of opportunity for some preventive intervention.

If you live in or visit an area with a lot of ticks, make sure to take precautions. Some of the newer flea products, specifically selamectin (Revolution) and fipronil (Frontline), have effects against some, but not all, species of ticks. Amitraz (Preventic) collars are also good for tick-infested areas, but it is a good idea to check with your veterinarian about what is recommended for your particular circumstances.

Internal Parasites

Sometimes what you can't see can be worse than what you do see. If you are living in close quarters with your dog, chances are that you'd like to keep canine cooties to a minimum. Studies have shown that internal parasites are present in a majority of dogs, even in the best cared-for pedigreed varieties. In fact, the problem is so prevalent (literally trillions of roundworm eggs alone are discharged into parks and yards every day) that routine parasite control should be considered de rigueur. Protocols vary, but medications are generally given to pups starting at two to three weeks of age, even before parasites are discharged in feces. You might think that two to three weeks of age is pretty young to start getting medicine, but keep in mind that treatment is for your safety, not that of your pup. The goal is to halt the spread of these internal parasites before they get discharged into the feces and become infective. Each year, some unlucky folks, usually children, end up in the hospital with parasites in their eyes (ocular larva migrans), in their livers (visceral larva migrans), or crawling under their skin (creeping eruption). It's not only disgusting but also entirely preventable.

Dogs also get roundworms, hookworms, and whipworms, but not pinworms. If you see something that looks like little grains of rice around your dog's anus, they're not pinworms—they are likely to be tapeworms. If you find tapeworms, your dog probably also has a problem with fleas, since that is how most species of tapeworm are transmitted. Dogs can also get *Giardia* spp and *Cryptosporidium* spp, and there is a good chance that these parasites can be circulated among family members. Now, that's gross!

For many dogs who live in areas with mosquitoes, heartworm medication is typically started by six months of age. Most of the newer preparations help control other internal parasites (more commonly known as worms) as well. A new product, moxidectin (ProHeart6), consists of one injection that gives six months of heartworm protection. It's also effective against hookworm. It's just getting easier to keep your dog parasite-free.

Worms aren't the only parasites that can cause problems, and under certain circumstances, owners can play pass-the-parasite with their pets. Organisms such as *Giardia* sp, *Cryptosporidium* sp, and entamoeba can be passed around to family members. The most likely scenario is not very appealing, but if you are aware of how these organisms are transmitted,

you can do a lot to nip the transmission in the bud. One quick solution is to keep your toilet lid down when you're not using it. Don't let your dog drink out of your toilet bowl. If you have a dog determined to nose open the lid for a cool drink, consider installing a toilet latch. You'll be taking a big step in preventing the perpetuation of parasites in your household, and you'll be much more receptive the next time your dog offers you a soft, wet kiss.

Medications

It may surprise you to know that many of the drugs used for dogs work effectively for people, too. Many of the very largest pharmaceutical companies, including Merck, Pfizer, American Home Products, and Novartis, have separate veterinary divisions. Drug development for animals often occurs parallel to human pharmaceutical research.

But while there are many similarities between people and dogs regarding medications, there are also significant differences of which you should be aware. Thus, while a drug such as fluoxetine HCl (Prozac), which is not licensed for use in animals, may be used by some veterinarians to manage certain conditions, other medications, such as acetaminophen (Tylenol), are not used in dogs and can actually be extremely toxic. Do not attempt to judge on your own which human drugs are safe for use in dogs. This is definitely a job for your veterinarian.

On the other hand, there are some wonderful medications available for dogs that have not yet made the transition to human medicine. For one thing, the parasite medicines that were alluded to earlier as being safe and effective for dogs are being used, on an experimental basis, in humans. In general, these products are far safer than most of the medicines currently used, and they work much better than the ones physicians are currently dispensing. Ideally, neither you nor anyone associated with you will have any of these parasite problems, but at some point in the future, the medications used to keep your dog parasite-free may start appearing in pharmacies for use in people.

Travel Advisory

For you take-your-dog-with-you travelers, do some homework about the area you are heading to. You may need to step up your parasite-control program, depending on where you plan to travel with your dog. If you're planning a beach trip to Florida, don't expect a flea-free experience. If you're heading for a hike in Connecticut, you need to be prepared for ticks that carry Lyme disease. A sojourn to Arizona may bring back an unwanted souvenir for the unprepared: ticks that carry ehrlichiosis (tick fever), or a potentially fatal fungal infection known as coccidioidomycosis, or valley fever. And, in any place with mosquitoes, heartworm can be anything but a heartwarming welcome. In summary, traveling with your canine pal can be much more fun when you take care of her medical needs before you head out the door.

Emergency, Emergency!

Once you've handled all the health-care basics and you're just concentrating on having fun with your dog, don't entirely forget the possibility of an emergency. In case an emergency occurs when you are not at home, always have printed information available that includes current vaccination records, the type and dosage of any current medications, and a run down of your dog's medical history filed from most current to oldest. Give a copy of this record to the person caring for your dog. Include contact information for your veterinarian as well as for an after-hours emergency clinic.

If there's a problem when you are home, don't panic. If you have a plan to follow, you will save time and possibly the life of your pet. Keeping a cool head is the first step in successfully resolving an emergency. Take time to carefully assess the situation.

While you may see a river of blood, the cause may be as simple as a torn nail that got caught on the carpet or on shrubbery. If your pet ingested something potentially poisonous, take the time to note the active ingredient in the product. Whether you deal with the ASPCA/National Animal Poison Control Center or a veterinary emergency clinic, the cause of the poisoning or details of the injury are critical to getting the proper treatment started as soon as possible. Some problems are definitely going to involve a trip to the veterinarian, but many others will just require you to be resourceful. There are some things you can do to make all the difference in the world.

When your dog is injured, you must also be aware of any aspects of the problem that may endanger your own safety. Remember that any dog, no matter how sweet or well trained, can lash out when in pain. Taking the time to assess the situation gives a better chance for a good outcome for everyone involved.

If you determine that your pet needs veterinary care, be aware of where emergency services are available. Your regular veterinary clinic may not be the closest, but if time is not too critical, it's the best place to be. It will have your pet's records and be familiar with any other medical conditions or treatments. If it is after hours, know where the nearest veterinary emergency center is. These facilities are fully staffed at times when most veterinary clinics are closed, typically evenings, weekends, and holidays. However, most are closed during regular business hours when veterinary hospitals are open.

If the situation is not too dire, you can probably handle most problems with a standard emergency first aid kit. Pet emergency kits are available, but there is not anything significantly different between pet kits and those intended for people. Whether you carry the kit as a fanny pack, in a carry bag, or in your car, the same kit is fine for any family member who needs treatment. Most of the time, a dab of antiseptic or a quick gauze wrap is all that your dog will need until you can contact your veterinarian for more specific advice.

Insurance

Whether you're confronted with an emergency or an unanticipated medical condition such as cancer or heart disease, dealing with the situation is often much easier if you have pet insurance. If you haven't heard of pet insurance, start doing your homework, because it is one of the best insurance deals you'll ever get. For whatever reason, only about 1 percent of pet owners carry pet health insurance, so it appears to be one of the best-kept secrets in pet health care. We're going to let you in on that secret!

Is a Pet Policy Right for You?

✔ Make sure the pet health company is licensed with your state's insurance department. Reputable companies must receive good-performance audits.

✔ Study what the policy covers and how much it pays for various treatments. Some plans allow each veterinary clinic to establish its own fee structure. Others have set amounts they'll pay, and these may differ from what your veterinarian charges.

✔ Ask about the plan's annual deductibles, which you must pay out of pocket.

✔ Read the fine print. Some policies exclude certain medical conditions.

✔ Contact your veterinarian to make sure that he or she accepts pet insurance policies. And make sure that the policy will accept bills from your veterinarian.

✔ See if the policy provides a preventive care package.

✔ Find out the time line for claim payments.

Prepare for a Natural Disaster

Twenty seconds. That's all it took for a tornado to rip open the roof, suck out the furniture, and send the door of the two-car garage hurtling a mile away.

When Jo Ann Eurell, D.V.M., her teenage son, Aaron, and their three dogs emerged from the safety of their interior bathroom, a mid-evening tornado had gutted their Urbana, Illinois, three-bedroom home. "It came up so quickly, and I was caught unprepared," says Dr. Eurell, a veterinarian and associate professor at the University of Illinois College of Veterinary Medicine, about the April 1996 tornado. "We got into the bathroom, and a minute later the tornado hit our house. We were barefoot. The dogs had no collars, no leashes. We're lucky to be alive."

Natural disasters can strike with or without warning. Before you're faced with an earthquake, hurricane, flood, wildfire, other wrath of Mother Nature, or a house fire, take steps now to protect your pet against injury, loss, or death. "There truly is no safe place in this country," says Cindy Lovern, D.V.M., assistant director for emergency preparedness and response for the American Veterinary Medical Association (AVMA) in Schaumburg, Illinois. "You need to be prepared beforehand because when a disaster strikes, you may have only minutes, seconds, to act, to evacuate your family and your pets." Dr. Lovern, who, along with her husband, a puppy, and two cats, survived a house fire in 1998, authored *Saving the Whole Family,* an AVMA disaster-preparedness booklet, in July 2000.

To obtain a free copy of *Saving the Whole Family* fax your request to (847) 925-1329 or mail your request to: AVMA, c/o Dr. Cindy Lovern, 1931 N. Meacham Road, Suite 100, Schaumburg, IL 60173.

The premiums are minuscule by human health care standards, nobody dictates which veterinarian you need to see, and most specialists and emergency facilities are also covered. There are many different insurance companies and policies out there, and it is important to understand what is covered and what isn't. It is also important to get your policy as soon as possible, before your dog gets sick and develops a pre-existing condition, which can be excluded from coverage. If you own a purebred, it's also important to understand which heritable conditions (e.g., hip dysplasia) might be excluded from coverage. When the unforeseen happens, insurance can provide you with peace of mind so you can make decisions without unduly focusing on your current financial situation.

So how do you find and choose an insurance plan? The best part about getting pet insurance is that you rarely have to deal with an insurance agent, and nobody is going to give you a sales pitch. Most of the policies can be ordered by mail, by telephone, or on the Internet. We've provided you with Web sites for most of the major insurance companies in Appendix B. Veterinarians don't sell the policies directly, but most have forms in their offices and can help pet owners select a policy that would be best for their circumstances.

Be prepared to review what each plan offers, because not all policies are alike, and not all companies actually sell insurance. Some are buyer's clubs that offer discounts on services, while others are full insurance companies, registered with insurance regulators in every state or province in which they sell policies.

Do yourself and your canine buddy a real favor and buy pet insurance now, without delay. It is the best bargain you will ever find in canine health care, and it's well worth the small amount of expense involved. In fact, if you are an employee at a large company, you might want to inquire as to whether pet health insurance is covered in your benefits.

According to a study by Metropolitan Life, pet insurance is the most requested corporate benefit after health and dental insurance. It never hurts to ask, but do it now. If you wait until your dog has a medical problem before you consider health insurance, you are already too late to take advantage of most of the benefits of coverage.

Follow these steps offered by the AVMA, before, during, and following a natural disaster

Before:

- ✔ Keep a current photo of your dog readily available on the refrigerator door or inside a pet carrier.
- ✔ Pack copies of your dog's vaccination records so that she can be admitted into pet-accepting shelters.
- ✔ Make sure your dog wears a collar with an ID tag that provides your phone number and your veterinarian's number. Better yet, have your veterinarian insert an ID microchip under your dog's skin.
- ✔ Select an appropriately sized pet carrier. It should be big enough for your dog to stand up and turn around in. Store an extra leash inside it.
- ✔ Keep a 15-day supply of dog food, water, and medications in airtight containers, stored in a cool, dry, easy-to-reach place in your home.
- ✔ Locate the safest spot in your home—one with interior walls that's big enough to house you, your family, and your pets during an earthquake, hurricane, or tornado.
- ✔ Identify pet-friendly shelters, veterinary clinics, friends, and other places where your dog could be housed temporarily if your home is destroyed.

During:

- ✔ Bring your dog indoors before a major storm strikes, if possible. Reassure and calm her.
- ✔ Usher your dog into a safe room in your house, pet carrier, or crate so that she will not try to dash outside during the disaster. Having your pet in her carrier will be handy if you have to make a quick evacuation with her.
- ✔ Bring a thick blanket or quilt into the bathroom or other safe place to use to cover you and your pets from flying glass and other debris.

After:

- ✔ Keep your dog on a leash, and watch where you walk because of downed power lines, debris, and other possible threats to your safety and that of your dog.
- ✔ Bring a photo of your lost dog to local animal shelters and veterinary clinics to help them recognize her.
- ✔ Monitor your dog's behavior after a storm. Some dogs become fearful, defensive, or aggressive.

CHAPTER 4

★ ★ ★ ★ ★ ★ ★ ★ ★

BEHAVIOR AND TRAINING TIPS FOR AN URBAN/SUBURBAN DOG

★ ★ ★ ★ ★ ★ ★ ★ ★

Thor keeps peeing on my living room carpet.

I'm at my wit's end. I can't stop Skipper from nipping ankles.

Rocket just chewed another shoe. That's the seventh one in a month.

Do any of the above scenarios sound too close to home? These are just three examples of telephone calls received by staff members operating an animal behavior help line at the Anti-Cruelty Society in Chicago. Every day, a dozen or more calls come from frustrated owners who are often just one step away from giving up hope and surrendering their dogs to local shelters.

When puppies pass the cute stage and enter the terrible twos, problems start developing, and people don't know how to deal with them. The top reasons people surrender dogs to shelters are behavioral problems. In fact, 30 percent of relinquishments are specifically linked to inappropriate behaviors that include hyperactivity, house soiling, destructive chewing, barking, growling, and biting. Often the owners are filled with guilt but see no other solution than surrendering their dog to a shelter or rescue group.

The best way to assure that your canine charge does not end up in a shelter is to concentrate on health-care, socialization, and training issues from the very start. If you don't want a dog because he has chewed up all your shoes, what makes you think anyone else would want to adopt him? The sad fact is that more dogs are killed each year for behavioral reasons than for *all* medical conditions combined.

Puppies and dogs aren't born trouble-seekers, scheming up ways to create havoc in our lives. Nor,

despite your experience, did you discover that your dog represents a new species: *Canis obnoxious*. If only you could wave a magic wand and—*poof!*—turn your dog into Mr. Manners, life would be less stressful for both of you. But dogs are not born with built-in manners and don't come with 100 percent–guaranteed training manuals. Their success as students depends on how well their owners fare as teachers.

These days, the majority of dogs live in suburbs and cities. They must interact with the rest of their household and community. In this chapter we offer positive and practical tools to stop your dog from excessive barking, begging, inappropriate chewing, and other unwanted behaviors.

Encouraging Good Behavior

Training begins the day you adopt your puppy or dog. It doesn't stop after he earns his certificate from puppy kindergarten or dog obedience class. Training needs to continue every day of your dog's

---

Good Behavior

What you need is the right tools—and the right attitude—to build the right relationship with your dog. Your Good Behavior Tool Kit should include:

✔ knowledge of how dogs communicate;

✔ a positive attitude that conveys you're clearly the household leader;

✔ an approach to training that rewards and reinforces good behavior;

✔ the ability to play doggy detective;

✔ recognition of the value of socializing your dog.

---

life. With this said, we're not suggesting that training become another time drain on your already busy schedule. The secret behind effective training is that you learn to blend learning sessions with your dog into your daily routine. Give an obedience command before your dog receives anything he desires or before he receives anything positive. For example, say, "sit," and have your dog sit before you give him a bowl of food. Apply this same sit cue before you give him attention, play with him, allow him to go out the door, and before other daily activities. You're instilling good manners in your dog so that they become a natural part of his actions.

LEARN TO INTREPRET HOW DOGS COMMUNICATE

The first step toward successful training is the recognition that people and dogs speak different languages. Too often what we view as ill manners are actually perfectly normal behaviors in the canine world. A classic example: during introductions, we shake hands; dogs sniff butts. People communicate primarily through words; dogs communicate more with body language. The folly comes when we misinterpret what our dogs are trying to tell us. Although postures may vary by breed and circumstance, here are some common body cue combinations to learn:

CLASSIC SIGNS OF A HAPPY, RELAXED DOG:

- Stands or sits with all four feet placed evenly on the ground
- Posture is free of muscle tension

- Forehead is smooth
- Eyes are narrowed or half-closed in a relaxed manner
- Mouth is relaxed at the corners or partly open as if smiling
- Floppy-eared breeds let their ears hang loosely, while breeds with pricked ears let them fall slightly outward

CLASSIC SIGNS OF AN AGGRESSIVE DOG:

- Ears forward
- Tail up and stiff, barely wagging
- Body tense and leaning forward
- Hair up on dog's shoulders and spine
- Prolonged staring
- Teeth bared from the front of the mouth

This Jack Russell terrier is relaxed.

CLASSIC SIGNS OF A SUBMISSIVE DOG:

- Ears back or flattened against the head
- Tail down or tucked between the legs
- Body shifted to the back legs
- Head lowered
- Makes indirect eye contact and quick glances
- May roll over and expose belly
- Lips pulled back in a submissive grin
- May crouch and urinate

"Dogtionary" Definitions

- ✔ **High-pitched bark:** The dog is lonesome or worried.
- ✔ **Quick, high-pitched, repetitive barks:** The dog wants to play or give chase.
- ✔ **Low, repetitive barks:** The dog feels protective or defensive toward the approach of someone, including a stranger.
- ✔ **A single bark or two:** The dog is saying, *Hey! I'm here and interested in what you're doing.*
- ✔ **Growling with teeth exposed and tense body leaning forward:** The dog is warning someone to back off.
- ✔ **Growling with body crouched low:** The dog is telling you that he is feeling defensive or afraid.
- ✔ **Singsong howling:** The dog is trying to contact others. This is a dog's version of the telephone.
- ✔ **Squeaky, repetitive yaps or whines.** The dog feels worried, scared, or stressed.

CLASSIC SIGNS OF A WORRIED OR ANXIOUS DOG:

- Dilated pupils
- Lips pulled back and creased at the corners
- Possible panting, a sure sign of stress
- Forehead muscles are tight and ears pulled back against the head

BE A POSITIVE LEADER

A second key tool in training is your attitude. Dogs are uncanny interpreters of our emotions. They know when we are angry, happy, or sad—but they don't usually know why. So when you come home and discover a puddle on your Persian rug and scold your dog, he knows you are angry but has no idea why. That mess on the rug may be due to a medical problem (urinary infections or a weak bladder, for instance), lack of proper house-training, or being kept indoors for 12 hours without the opportunity to go outside to potty.

It is vital that you establish yourself as the leader of the household pack—not by brute force but by consistently setting clear household rules. A dog doesn't mind being at the bottom rung on the household hierarchy. He will get bugged when he doesn't know his position or if he senses confusion among others within the household. He looks to you to set the social ranking. A dog who views you as number one feels safe knowing you're in charge. In turn, you need to be the one who sets the rules of the household: feeding time, playtime, work time. You need to set when activities begin and when they end. Not your dog. A dog bucking for control of the family will start seeking more and more attention. If you respond to his every whim—or whine—he'll quickly think, *Hey, looks like she wants me to be in charge. She'd better start obeying MY orders.*

BE POSITIVE WITH YOUR TRAINING

A third essential tool is to rely on a proper training technique. Positive reinforcement is the healthiest—and most effective—approach to training your dog: out with the word *no* and in with the word *yes*. Negative training, which includes slapping, swatting with a rolled-up newspaper, jerking on the leash, screaming, shaking, or pinning a dog to the floor, seldom works and is harmful and hurtful. Sure, these actions may interrupt the bad behavior for a second or two as your dog stops and turns to see what's going on, but rarely do these forms of punishment provide a permanent fix. These negative forms of punishment can often worsen a dog's fear response and heighten his level of anxiety. They can also sever the trust and friendship between you and your dog.

The use of physical punishment can come back to haunt you by giving your dog the wrong message. Let's say your dog starts pulling on the leash to check out an approaching person. In response, you jerk hard on the leash and yell, "Bad dog!" Your dog may interpret that signal to mean either he is being bad for pulling on the leash or that the person he wanted to approach is bad. And some dogs actually perceive punishment as a reward. If your dog barks when you host your weekly dinner party and you

banish him to the back bedroom, your dog may think, *Great, finally a place of safety. Now I know how to act the next time I want to get away from these visitors.*

You can shape a dog's behavior by reinforcing desired actions and ignoring unwanted behaviors in what psychologists refer to as operant conditioning. Dogs learn by association. Naturally, a dog is apt to repeat an action (such as digging in the yard) when it leads to a satisfying result (getting cool during a hot summer day). The principle behind operant conditioning states that if an action leads to a satisfying result, the action will be repeated.

Use this principle to your advantage. You may have thought it was cute when your 4-pound puppy jumped on people when they arrived at the front door, but now your puppy is a weighty 50-pound, overly excited adult who is knocking over visitors. The solution: Train your dog to sit automatically at the door when greeting people.

Let's say your Labrador jumps and nearly knocks you off your feet with exuberance each time you walk in the front door. This is his way of saying how glad he is to see you. Telling him no sternly or pushing him away seems only to motivate him to jump even more because you are giving him attention—to a dog, even negative attention is better than no attention at all.

To decrease your dog's jumping tendencies, you need to stop rewarding this inappropriate action. The solution: Give him the cold shoulder. When you come in the door and he comes bounding your way,

This person is encouraging her dog to jump up on people when greeting them by giving him attention.

turn your back and ignore him when he jumps on you. When he sits pretty, give him praise and even a food treat. In time, your dog will put two and two together: *Hmmm…when I jump on her, she ignores me. When I sit, she gives me a friendly pat and a biscuit. I think I'll start sitting more.* If your dog is not motivated by food, identify the toy that he loves the best and use that toy to shape good behavior.

Gradually expand this concept to include all visitors. Keep a small treat jar (with a lid on it) near the front door. Instruct your guests to give your dog a treat from this jar when he politely sits to greet them. Your dog will evolve from an obnoxious jumper into a four-footed doorman in no time!

We also recommend the practice of rewarding an incompatible behavior. Yes, it sounds confusing, but the fact is a dog can't feel happy and sad at the same moment. It's impossible. Use this knowledge to your advantage by rewarding your dog for a desired behavior that is incompatible with an unacceptable one. Let's say your dog insists on barking at other dogs during your evening walk. When you see other dogs on leashes approach, quickly divert your dog's attention by putting him in the sit position. Have him make eye contact with you. When he does, give him a food treat. A dog looking for that tasty treat will be less apt to bark at other dogs because there is no reward for that action. He will soon learn what behaviors reap the tastiest dividends.

An important obedience command you should teach your dog is leave it. By teaching your dog to obey those two words, you will save yourself from many problems. If you drop food on the floor that you don't want your dog to gobble up, rather than leaping to retrieve it before your quick-as-lightning Jack Russell terrier moves in, you can stay in your chair and simply say, "leave it."

The "leave it" command is easy to teach. Start by having your dog in a sit position and on a leash. Keep a stash of his favorite treats cut into small pieces in your pocket. Place a treat of lesser value on the floor. Walk your dog on his leash passed the floor treat, saying "leave it" as he walks by it. If he lunges for the treat on the floor, use your leash to steer him out of reach. Reward him with praise each time he "ignores" this dropped food and at the end of the training session, have him sit and give him a few of the higher premium treats from your pocket.

Another must-know command is to train your dog to come when you call his name. The key to successful recalls is to always reinforce compliance of this command with positive praise or treats. Dogs sometimes behave in less-than-ideal ways because their owners fail to be consistent in their commands. If you call your dog to come and praise and pet him each time he responds, he is likely to obey, perhaps even more quickly the next time you call for him.

Taking your dog to a dog-friendly beach is something both of you can enjoy.

But if you call him by name and, on occasion, yell at him for tipping over the kitchen garbage can, he may be less likely to heed your come command the next time he hears it. He will associate the sound of his name and the word come with a negative consequence: a scolding. Never, ever call your dog over to you and then scold him for running away or doing something wrong. Your dog will quickly associate the word come with punishment, and not with happy greetings from his owner. The beauty is that you can teach most dogs these essential commands in a few quick lessons and enjoy the benefits for the dog's entire lifetime.

Always keep in mind that dogs possess great memories. For example, a dog may learn to detest car rides if the only times he is in the car are when he is headed for the veterinary clinic or being dropped off for an overnight stay at a boarding kennel. You need to introduce positive road trips with your dog from day one by taking him along on short errands, to dog parks, to dog-friendly beaches, or for overnight stays at your dog-loving friends' homes. In time, your dog will learn to associate the car with fun activities so that the occasional trip to the veterinary clinic will be tolerated better.

PLAY DOG DETECTIVE

A fourth training tool is recognizing that dogs usually have a good reason for their behaviors. If your dog is acting up, play dog detective and try to pinpoint the cause behind the unwanted behavior. A dog who ignores your calls, for instance, may have an ear infection or be in the early stages of cognitive dysfunction syndrome, the doggy equivalent of dementia or Alzheimer's disease in people. Your dog may feel lost, even like a stranger in his own house. When in doubt, have your dog examined by your veterinarian to consider any possible underlying medical cause behind an inappropriate behavior.

Let's say your dog is deemed physically fit but continues to bark excessively. Try to determine when your dog barks. Is there a pattern such as barking only during thunderstorms or on Monday mornings? When did the barking pattern begin: when he was a puppy or recently? Did it start after you moved into a new home, when you returned from a long vacation, or after your daughter left for college? Where does your dog bark: inside, outside, or both? Does he bark at everything and anyone, or at just a specific person or object? Taking the time to pay attention to the factors that seem to cause barking might help you come up with a solution.

When you take your dog on positive road trips he will learn to like riding in the car.

Solutions for Common Doggy Misdeeds

Dogs will be dogs—if you let them. Terry Ryan, a world-recognized professional dog trainer from Sequim, Washington, and author of *The Toolbox for Remodeling Your Problem Dog,* offers these helpful tactics for five common dog misdeeds:

1. **Leash tugging:** Your dog drags you during your daily walks and yanks and lunges after other dogs, squirrels, or cats.

   Quick solution: Train your dog to walk with manners by the use of a head halter such as a Gentle Leader Headcollar, Halti, or Softee. These collars are more effective and humane than choke or pinch collars. The halters allow you to control your dog's head, which in turn controls where his body will go. During walks, reward your dog with praise or a small food treat any time there is slack in the leash. Refuse to continue the walk when he starts to pull. "If you control the head, you control the dog," says Ryan. "A head halter does not put pressure on your dog's throat. It fits up higher and rests on the jawbones to give you physical control without hurting your dog. It also gives you psychological control because most dogs recognize the muzzle strap as an extension of your leadership and will often settle into a more mellow mood once they are wearing it."

   At the same time, increase your own "curb appeal" with your easily distracted dog. Before you head out for a walk, stash a few yummy treats or your dog's favorite toy in your jacket. Periodically call your dog by name during your stroll. When he pays attention to you, give him a treat or play a quick game of fetch. Then continue the walk. This will increase your popularity over that empty candy wrapper in the gutter or other distractions during your walk together.

2. **Inappropriate chewing:** Your dog destroys your shoes, wallet, television remote control, socks, or other prized possessions.

   Quick solution: Become a tidier housekeeper. Store wallets and socks in dresser drawers, remotes on high shelves, and shoes in closets with doors or in rooms closed off with baby gates. Divert your dog's attention to his chew toys, which may be a hollow rubber Kong or Buster Cube. Stuff the Kong with peanut butter or cream cheese and fill the Buster Cube with pieces of kibble to increase the value of these toys. Your dog will prefer these tasty treats to the mundane black sock.

3. **Garden digging:** No need to sacrifice your strawberry patch or herb garden to your dog's desire to dig like a gold miner.

   Quick solution: First, protect your garden areas by installing a low but sturdy fence to make it off-limits to your dog. Then provide a sandbox with occasional buried treats or toys for your dig-happy dog. Also consider installing a dog run or outdoor kennel. You can purchase a premade steel-and-wire dog run from many pet supply stores.

4. **Trash can tipping:** The smell of last night's steak and potato scraps in the kitchen garbage can be too irresistible to your dog, whom you might discover head-deep in the can with trash strewn across the floor.

   Quick solution: Take away the temptation by storing the trash can and its smelly treasures out of paw's reach. Place the trash bin in the cabinet under the sink, and install an inexpensive childproof latch on the cabinet doors. Or buy a trash can with either a snap-on lid or one you can clamp down using bungee cords. You can also stow the trash can inside the garage, or install a baby gate in your kitchen doorway to block your dog's access.

5. **Furniture lounging:** Does your hairy dog insist on draping himself over your recliner, stretching out on your sofa, or commandeering your loveseat when you're not home?

   Quick solution: If possible, turn recliners upside down and up against walls while you're away from home. Place a cookie sheet over a chair to make it less inviting, or compromise by placing a washable blanket or sheet over the furniture to allow your dog to snooze with comfort. Remove the covering when you return home at night. Consider providing a doggy bed in the living room. Some fashion-conscious dog owners choose doggy beds that match the patterns and colors of their furniture.

INTRODUCE YOUR DOG TO THE SOCIAL SCENE

A final training tool is proper socialization. We're not advocating that you turn your dog into a party animal, but he does need to be exposed to different people, pets, places, and noises to help him learn how to act in a variety of situations and settings. Socialization is as important to a dog's development as regular medical examinations, nutritionally balanced meals, and daily exercise.

The younger you can introduce your puppy to different sights, sounds, and smells in a safe way, the better he will grow into a well-adjusted adult. Veterinarians and animal behaviorists agree that between 5 to 12 weeks of age, puppies enter what's known as the socialization period. This is the prime time for a developing puppy to learn proper doggy etiquette and how to interact with littermates, people, and other animals. That explains the growing popularity of puppy kindergarten classes.

Professional dog trainer Bryon Davies conducts formal puppy classes in Middletown, Rhode Island. She relies on positive reinforcement techniques so that learning is fun for the puppies and their family members. Mistakes are ignored, and successes are praised and rewarded with tasty bite-sized treats. "Puppies are so eager. They're practically begging to learn," says Davies. "This is a great time to build appropriate behaviors in your dog."

Yes, you should enroll your puppy in these organized classes, but also incorporate little socialization sessions every day while at home or out and about

with your young dog. Once your puppy has had his second round of vaccinations, consider spending thirty minutes or so on a park bench with him. His cuteness will quickly attract all types of people of all ages. He will get a lot of praise and attention, but more importantly, the little database in his brain will be filing away positive associations with little children, men with beards, women wearing hats, and so on.

Outings to Hone Your Puppy's Socialization Skills

✔ Bring your puppy with you to an outdoor cafe. Sip your favorite beverage while your puppy takes in all the sights, sounds, and smells. Be sure to pack a portable bowl, a plastic bottle of water, and a few tasty treats for your puppy.

✔ Take your puppy on quick errands to pick up dry cleaning, do drive-through banking, or order lunch from a fast-food restaurant. These outings will build up your puppy's view of the car as something positive.

While socialization deals with relationships, it is also important to acclimate your dog of any age to different surroundings. This is referred to in behavioral lingo as habituation. Expose your dog to different surfaces such as grass, sidewalks, hiking trails, snow, and even slick surfaces such as the tops of washing machines. Introduce him to different smells such as flowers, a steak on the grill, and freshly scrubbed floors. Bring him to different places such as dog parks, beaches, busy city streets, and quiet outdoor cafes.

Enroll your older dog in obedience classes or performance sports classes such as agility or flyball. Instill good manners in a dog of any age and any breed by enrolling him in the American Kennel Club's (AKC's) Canine Good Citizen Program. Graduates of this course learn how to accept an approach by a friendly stranger, sit politely to be petted, walk nicely on a leash, maneuver calmly through a crowd, sit and stay on command, come when called, behave politely around other dogs, deal with distractions, and stay when temporarily separated from their owners. To find a class in your area, you can contact the AKC by calling (919) 852-3875 or tapping into its Web site, www.akc.org, or you can ask your veterinarian, groomer, animal shelter, or local breed club.

The Truth About Dogs and Kids

To ensure a good relationship between your dog and your children, we offer these suggestions:

- **Spay or neuter your puppy before the age of six months.** Sterilized pets are less prone to certain cancers and hormone-induced aggressiveness.
- **Create safe childproof havens and escape routes for your dog.** Place your dog in a room barricaded by see-through door gates, rather than behind closed doors, when you need to give him some time away from young children. Being able to view family activity from a safe place helps reduce any anxiety-related tendencies in your dog.
- **Send your dog to school.** Dogs need to learn four basic commands: *sit, down, stay,* and *come*. Practice these commands in the presence of your

children so that your dog learns that children rank higher than they do in the family hierarchy and should be treated with respect. Always offer praise and a food treat each time your dog dutifully performs the requested command. Teach your older children how to practice these commands with your dog.

- **Teach your children some doggy manners.** Make it a household rule that no one should disturb your dog when he is eating, sleeping, or chewing on treats or toys. Teach your children not to run and scream around your dog, blow in his face, or give him full body hugs.
- **Enlist the aid of your children in dog duties.** Children under the age of 5, though still in the "me-me-me" phase of cognitive development, can serve as your helpful apprentices by giving your dog a treat for good behavior or helping you fill a water or food bowl. By the age of 7, children should learn never to hit, kick, or throw objects at a dog or other animal. By the age of 12, children can handle daily feeding and watering duties, walking the dog, and joining you at obedience or sports classes for your dog.
- **Identify fun dog-children interactive games.** Do not play games like tug-of-war, wrestling, and chase with a dog because you are inadvertently teaching the dog that you like it when he fights with you, and he may end up biting you or your child. Instead, encourage your children to play interactive games of fetch, find it, and hide-and-seek with your dog. All these games value team-

By the age of 12, children can handle many of the daily dog duties.

work, not competition. Instruct your children to praise the dog and give him treats to make this a fun activity for all.

- **Supervise your dog around infants and children.** Never leave your dog alone with a baby or toddler. Even if you own what you view as the world's friendliest dog, don't risk the safety of your children or your dog. Your child may accidentally fall on your sleeping dog, startling him and causing him to possibly react by biting.

Let's Get Acquainted

Do you absolutely adore every person you meet? Hardly. Like us, dogs are socially minded, but they also have their favorites when it comes to other dogs, cats, and people. Introductions are key, and that's where you enter the scene.

When introducing your dog to another dog (who may or may not join your household), we recommend choosing a neutral turf so that your dog won't view this newcomer as a territorial intruder. Both dogs should be on leashes. You hold your dog's leash, and someone else maintains control of the other dog. Let the two dogs sniff each other (a normal canine greeting) while you speak in a friendly, positive tone. After ten seconds or so, separate the dogs and give each of them treats for obeying a *sit* or *stay* command. Then walk the dogs, keeping them apart. Occasionally stop to allow them to sniff each other. Provide more treats.

Your goal here is to create a good mood to encourage the dogs to be friendly. Watch their body postures. Things are going well if they go into what's called a play bow (front legs on the ground, head lowered, and back end raised high in the air). If either dog is emitting deep growls or an icy stare, disrupt the dogs by calmly and positively calling them, having them sit, and giving them a treat to avoid these gestures from escalating into acts of aggression.

Once the dogs appear to be pals, bring them home for the second round of introductions. Initially, give preference for treats and toys to the resident dog but realize that in time, dogs will establish their own social ranking.

Nixing Noise Phobias

If many dogs had their way, they would paw the mute button on thunderstorms, vacuum cleaners, fireworks, and other noisy sounds. The intense booms and bangs of fireworks and storms, and the high-pitched whines of household appliances can transform mellow dogs into fear-filled canines. In efforts to escape these sounds, some dogs panic by crashing through plate glass windows, chewing through walls, and leaping over backyard fences.

Larry Lachman shares the story of Fagan, his beloved golden retriever, now deceased. She basically ignored holiday fireworks for three years. Then, without warning, she suddenly panicked during the fourth year. "Fagan freaked out and just starting shaking, then drooling, crying, hyperventilating, and eventually was trying to dig a hole to hide in," recalls Dr. Lachman, an animal behavior consultant. Fagan's fireworks fear was not addressed, resulting in the dog developing fright reactions to other sounds, such as a rolling thunderstorm, someone tapping a stick against a tree, or a cork popping from a champagne bottle.

What to Look for in a Trainer

Say you've just adopted a puppy and want to get him off on the right paw by enrolling him in a top-notch puppy kindergarten class. Or you have a "problem dog" who needs a refresher course in manners and obedience. Or you just attended your

---

Tips on How to Restore Calmness and Confidence in Noise-Sensitive Dogs

✔ Convert an interior room of your house into a calm sanctuary for your dog. Bring in your dog's favorite toy and one of your lived-in T-shirts as comfort during an approaching thunderstorm.

✔ Shut the windows, close the blinds, and draw the curtains.

✔ Turn on the air conditioner and television or radio to muffle outside sounds.

✔ Set aside time in the late morning of July Fourth to exercise your dog. Depending on the health and preference of your dog, take him for a long run or swim, or engage him in a game of fetch, agility, or some other energy-burning activity so that he will be tired and wanting to snooze when the fireworks show starts. Walk your dog on a leash a couple of hours before dusk so that he can relieve his bladder before the firecrackers start to explode. Wait until an hour after the fireworks to take your dog out for his final bathroom break of the night.

✔ Close the doggy door so your dog cannot try to leap out in a panic during a storm or fireworks show.

✔ Distract your dog by engaging in one of his favorite indoor games or by offering him a chew toy stuffed with peanut butter or one of his favorite foods.

✔ Reward confident behavior and avoid comforting or soothing fearful behavior, which will only reinforce the fear.

✔ Desensitize your dog's fears of the vacuum cleaner, water hose, lawn mower, and other appliances. Put your dog in another part of your home before you begin using the targeted appliance. Keep him inside an enclosed room or one with a baby gate. To desensitize your dog to the appliance, slowly increase your dog's exposure to it (first with it turned off and at a distance). Then gradually move the appliance closer and closer over time. Monitor your dog's reaction at each step; it may be necessary to repeat a step until your dog demonstrates consistent confidence. Eventually turn the appliance on in your dog's presence. Reward him with food treats and praise each time he remains calm around it.

If you feel that you're striking out when it comes to teaching appropriate behavior to your dog, don't hesitate to seek professional help from veterinarians, trainers, or animal behaviorists. More and more animal shelters are offering pet parenting classes and behavior help lines to turn your frightened Fido into a fun-loving, well-mannered dog.

---

first agility dog event and are eager to compete with your high-energy dog. You realize that you need a professional dog trainer, but how do you make the right choice for you and your dog? View dog trainer selection with the same regard you devote to choosing a new car. In other words, do your homework. Find a trainer who is current with reward-based training techniques, not the outdated negative punishment approach.

A skilled dog trainer will:

✔ provide a clear explanation of each lesson, covering how you do each step as well as why you are doing it;

✔ first demonstrate the behaviors, using a trained dog or a dog from the class so the class can see how to do it;

✔ distribute written handouts that provide step-by-step instructions for owners to practice with their dogs at home;

✔ use positive reinforcement to direct an owner and his or her dog to the appropriate behavior or technique.

In selecting a trainer, consider these eight vital points:

1. **Evaluate the class environment for safety.** Beginners classes, for instance, should cover the basics in a fun, cooperative approach and not require dogs to perform advanced or complex commands. The location should provide adequate lighting if indoors and should have shade if outdoors to keep the dogs from getting overheated.

2. **Find out the instructor's credentials.** The best professional dog trainers own dogs and are willing to showcase their good manners to the class. Seek a trainer who keeps current on training methods by enrolling in continuing education programs or one who serves as a judge for a dog activity such as agility.

3. **Attend a couple of classes as an observer before deciding to enroll.** Qualified trainers encourage individuals considering their classes to watch a few from the sidelines. Attend the first class without your dog so that you can devote your full attention to seeing how the trainer motivates people and their dogs, the mood of the class, and the level of interaction between the students and the trainer. Then bring your dog to a class, on a leash, and watch together. Watching will help give you a true idea of the physical demands required for both you and your dog.

4. **Pay attention to the size of the class.** Ideally, the class should be limited in size so that you get ample time to practice new techniques with your dog and not waste a lot of time standing around and waiting your turn. Does it seem like too few or too many dogs? Are you comfortable with the ratio of instructors to dogs? Are there assistants who can handle administrative duties so that the trainer can devote his or her entire attention to teaching the class? Do you feel that your dog would receive enough one-on-one attention?

5. **Avoid classes that last more than 90 minutes.** Dogs, especially puppies, have a short attention span. Stick with trainers who limit their classes to 90 minutes or less so the canine classmates can maintain focus.

6. **Heed the comments and reactions of students.** Do owners appear to be relaxed and enjoying the class? Are their comments positive or negative when they leave class? Does the trainer encourage owners to bring in their older children and other dog caregivers to participate, or is the class limited to just one owner per dog?

7. **Schedule a time to interview the instructor.** Find out what training methods an instructor uses and why before deciding on a specific instructor. Avoid trainers who rely on negative techniques such as yanking on choke chains or leashes. Also sidestep those who guarantee results. You need to match an instructor's training style with what will work for your dog. A reputable trainer is willing to spend twenty minutes or more with you without any interruptions. A good trainer also has good communication skills and is able to clearly convey tips and techniques to students.

8. **Respect your dog's instincts.** Dog classes require a partnership between you and your dog. Your dog must like the trainer to be willing to learn. A willing canine student rushes to greet his trainer with a back wiggle and wide tail-sweeping motions. A reluctant or fearful dog will crouch and tuck in his tail each time the trainer approaches.

To help you find a qualified dog trainer in your area, we recommend that you contact the Association of Professional Dog Trainers (APDT) in Springfield, New Jersey, at (800) PET-DOGS.

Walk away if a dog trainer:

✔ instructs you to pin your dog on his back and loom over him in a dominating stance. This can actually backfire and lead to aggression in some dogs;

✔ strongly urges you put a choke chain on your dog and pull on it to correct an unwanted behavior or action. Pain-induced learning can harm your dog;

✔ tells you to yank sharply on your dog's leash and lift his front feet off the ground to stop an unwanted action.

Tips on Choosing an Animal Behaviorist

There may be a time when you'll reach the point at which you'll need one-on-one professional help to modify unwanted—or potentially dangerous—behaviors in your dog. That's when a professional animal behaviorist may be necessary to restore harmony in your household. Seek a behaviorist who uses positive methods, agrees to see you and your dog in person instead of prescribing a solution over the telephone, and is willing to provide you with a list of client references.

CHAPTER 5

* * * * * * * *

SELECTING
PET ALLIES

* * * * * * * *

When it comes to spending time with your canine pal, do you ever feel like an absentee dog parent? With job demands, the long commute, and family tugs, twelve hours or more often lapse before you return home at the end of a yet another long day. As you usher your weary self inside to flop into the recliner, your path becomes blocked by your raring-to-go, tail-thumping dog, eager to break up the monotony of yet another boring day spent home alone. The guilt barometer inside you rises and your heart sinks as you utter, "Sorry, pal, not right now." You promised you would play fetch with her tonight, but you're too exhausted. Last Tuesday's scheduled trip to the dog park got sidetracked when your boss tossed a must-be-ready-by-tomorrow project on your desk. Your dog is sporting a hippie-looking hair coat that smells oh-too-much like dog, but you haven't found time in your daily schedule to drop her off at the groomers and pick her up later in the day.

Keep in mind that dogs are social animals who crave—and need—interaction with people and other pets. They are full-fledged members of the family. In fact, a national survey by the American Animal Hospital Association reports that 9 out of 10 owners consider their dogs family members, and 3 out of 4 feel guilty when they must leave their dogs home alone. Ideally, dogs shouldn't go more than five hours in a row without any human contact during the day—but can withstand

Dogs shouldn't go more than five hours a day without human contact.

Consider putting your dog in doggy day care so she doesn't have to be home alone all day.

eight hours tops. In reassessing your situation, ask yourself if your dog is truly happy being home alone with a chew toy and free access to the sofa.

You truly love and adore your dog but chide yourself for being a poor pet parent. What you need are allies—professional doggy delegates who can cater to your canine's needs and save you time and guilt. And you could use a little bit of time management to maximize your fun with your dog and mini-mize any feelings of guilt. Help is here and getting better and more versatile by the day. Pet care as an industry is growing exponentially to fill the growing demands of time-squeezed dog owners. What were regarded one or two decades ago as novelties—doggy day care centers and dog summer camps—are now hailed as essential godsends.

Initially, you may be concerned about the dollars you're doling out for your dog. We suggest a different

Older children who are home alone often find comfort in having a dog around.

mind-set: Think of your dog as your child. Would you leave your 10-year-old home alone? Of course not. Would you search diligently to find a quality day care or after-school program with a professional staff that meets your child's needs? Certainly. Apply this same dogged determination for your canine, especially if you need to be gone for more than eight hours a day.

While we are well aware that sometimes children are left at home alone, the latchkey phenomenon is a troubling one. If you do have older children who need to be left at home while you work, do errands, or are busy being a soccer mom for other children in the family, sometimes the child-dog combination is a better alternative for both dependents. According to authors Thomas and Lynette Long in their book *The Handbook for Latchkey Children and Their Parents*, the most common fear of children left home alone is that someone will break in and hurt them. On the other hand, older home-alone children who are bored and lonely are much more likely to get into trouble. The solution may be just the answer to your dog's prayers. Molly doesn't mind being the guardian of the household, and this should be reassuring for the older kids. Children usually don't mind pet-related chores, which should be just fine for Molly (and a great relief and time-saver for you).

We certainly don't recommend leaving children or dogs for long stretches of time, but we are aware of the realities of everyday life. If you don't have a child who would benefit from canine companionship, you probably don't have to look far in the neighborhood for a child who needs something to do after school. You could create a mutually beneficial arrangement. In any case, children benefit from the responsibility of daily duties, and it doesn't do dogs any harm to have someone play with them!

So, when leaving the house, remember to assign everyone appropriate duties during the time you'll be away. Sophie's job is to be ever vigilant and make sure the house remains safe during your absence. The children may be assigned duties such as brushing Sophie making sure she has clean, fresh water, and perhaps even doing some basic obedience work. If you think it is safe, and if the weather is appropriate, this could also be the time for both to get their exercise with a nice walk. After all, depending on the circumstances, getting out of the house is a great way to reduce anxiety and that uncomfortable feeling of being alone. Both should be entitled to a healthy snack when chores have been successfully completed, and perhaps some snuggling on the couch for a job well done. Time-consuming chores such as these help assure that neither child nor dog has too much idle time in which to get into trouble. It may not be the perfect solution to the latchkey problem, but it is better for child and dog to have each other than to be alone. Think about it!

Dogs who are left home alone for 12-hour stretches can start to exhibit signs of loneliness— incessant barking, potty presents, destructive chewing, and other behavioral whines for help. In the end, it will cost you more—in terms of money and time—to correct those bad behaviors.

Professional dog walkers can be a great alternative if you are unable to do it yourself.

sniffs of the fire hydrant will clue her in on what dog—specifically, sex, age, and size—had left his or her calling card on the hydrant prior to her arrival. There are people to meet and greet on the sidewalk, birds to eye and admire, and the sounds of honking horns to absorb. And if your dog is lucky, she gets the opportunity for a nose-to-head introduction of another canine while out and about. Busy, busy, busy. When she returns home from a 30-minute walk, she is filled with a lot of new sensations and experiences that add to her social skill–building repertoire.

If you don't have time to walk your dog twice a day every day, consider hiring a professional dog walker. Dog walkers first became popular in New York City decades ago. Today, owning a dog and hiring a walker is becoming more of the norm in Manhattan. But dog walkers are no longer limited to major metropolitan areas. More and more professional dog striders are operating businesses in the suburbs. You get the peace of mind of knowing that your dog will be given a vigorous, calorie-burning trek and will have an activity to fill her otherwise snooze-on-the-sofa day. She will be in better shape—both physically

Are you ready to be a good pet parent? Let's take a closer look at the advantages of enlisting the aid of some pet allies.

Dog Walkers

There is more to a dog walk than a quick bathroom trip. Put yourself in your dog's paws for a moment. A walk to a dog is a major social event. A couple of and mentally—thanks to these regular walks. Dog walkers offer flexibility and a willingness to accommodate your schedule.

We recommend using dog walkers who are licensed, insured, and bonded. Make sure that you select walkers who transport dogs in safe, well-ventilated vehicles, who use humane handling methods (no leash popping or yanking), and who clean up feces left by their canine clientele. They should be willing to meet your dog at your home and should ask for detailed information about her care. During outings, your dog should wear a collar with an identification tag and be current on her necessary vaccinations.

The cost of this time-saving service depends on the length of the walk and where you live, but expect the price to range from $10 to $25 per day. Ask if the walker offers discounts if you buy a month's worth of walking. Interview prospective walkers and ask for references. Talk with others who rely on their walking services before you decide.

A good question to ask is how many dogs they walk at one time. This is a case where more is not better, especially if you have a shy dog. We've seen walkers deftly handling six leashed dogs on a side-

walk simultaneously, but that's a situation prime for calamity. One stray cat can suddenly appear, and the chase is on. Insist that your dog walk solo or be paired with a canine pal.

Doggy Nannies

For those wishing for someone who will do more than walk their dogs, we suggest a couple of options: professional pet sitters or doggy day care. Both are attractive alternatives for a stay-behind dog. Many owners are finding that they like mixing up their dog's weekday by hiring a pet sitter for three days and sending their dog to day care for two days. See what works best for you and your dog.

PET SITTERS

We salute people like Patti Moran. Back in 1994, she had the vision to see the need for an extra pair of dog-friendly helping hands in many American households. She created Pet Sitters International, an organization that now has more than 3,800 members in all 50 states plus 10 Canadian provinces and 10 countries. One toll-free telephone call to (800) 268-SITS or a few keystrokes on the computer keyboard (www.petsit.com) and you can be paired with a professional pet sitter from your area who is licensed, bonded, insured, and pet-savvy. Make sure that the pet sitter provides written proof of commercial liability insurance, offers local references (from veterinarians and clients), and gives you a brochure that describes his or her services and spells out all fees. You can hire a dog sitter to spend an hour or so in the middle of the day to walk your dog, but pet sitters do more than walk, feed, and play with your dog. Some are also willing to take care of other household needs if you must be gone overnight or longer. Depending on your arrangement, some will bring in the mail and newspaper, water the plants, stay in your home, and even take your dog to the veterinarian or groomer. Pet sitters are also trained to give dogs medication, and they know how to reach emergency veterinarians quickly should an unexpected mishap occur. And if you do have to be away overnight, your dog gets the benefit of being able to stay at home, surrounded by her familiar smells, sights, and sounds—including her favorite toys and your smelly T-shirt.

How do you know which pet sitter is right for you? Interview several, and let your dog make the final vote. Reputable sitters will arrange for a get-acquainted visit. Use this opportunity to gauge how your dog reacts to each sitter. Does your dog back away or want to leap in the sitter's lap? Also, watch how the sitter communicates with your dog. Does he or she speak in soothing, confident tones? We recommend that you hire two sitters—one as a backup in case the first is unavailable at a time you need to be away.

DOGGY DAY CARE

Want to put a smile on your lonely dog's face? Arrange for her to spend a day or more each week at a doggy day care center. Unlike a child day care center, doggy day care won't teach your dog her ABCs, but it will give her the chance to strengthen her social skills, perhaps practice her basic obedience commands, and unleash her pent-up energy—all under the watchful supervision of trained dog professionals. Contact your local animal shelter, groomer, or veterinarian for the names of day care centers in your area.

Credit a devoted dog owner for coming up with the concept of doggy day care. Joe Sporn of New York City is credited with creating the first doggy day care back in January 1987 when he was a veterinary technician and college student looking for a fun place for his German shepherd dog puppy, Valkyrie, to stay while he was working. "I am the first, I claimed it, and no one has ever disputed my claim," says Sporn, who has been profiled in newspapers, including the *New York Times*. Unable to find a place for his high-energy puppy, Sporn decided to create a canine version of child day care. He relied on word-of-mouth advertising about his indoor-outdoor place, located on the ground floor of a five-story building in a residential neighborhood adjacent to a commercial district of New York City. Today his doggy day care center caters to 20-25 dogs a day and is open seven days a week from 6:45 A.M. to 8:00 P.M. year-round. All dogs are temperament tested and are current on their necessary shots.

Although there is not a national professional doggy day care association yet, Sporn estimates there are about five hundred doggy day care centers in the United States. The number is growing steadily as more owners realize the value of socialization for their canine pals. "Doggy day care is a fast-growing industry," says Sporn. "Owners are realizing that dogs are pack animals that need to be socialized around other dogs and people. And it is vital on the part of business owners in the pet industry to cater to the needs of dogs and their owners."

To help you select the day care that best meets your dog's needs, we offer this checklist:

- Schedule an appointment to visit the center with your dog on a leash.
- Is the staff willing to give you a complete tour of the facility? Be leery of centers in which employees are reluctant to show you where the dogs rest, lounge, or play.
- Compare the size of the center with the number and size of the dogs. Is the space ample or too small? Also compare the ratio of dogs to staff.
- Check the cleanliness of the center. Does it smell clean or emit urine and doggy odors? Are the floors free of debris and balls of fur? Does it have an on-site washer and dryer?
- Examine the layout. Does the center provide an outdoor play area? If there is no outdoor area, where and how do dogs relieve themselves?
- Are there separate interior areas for play, lounging, and nap times? How are small and larger dog guests separated?
- How safe and secure is the center? Are there double doors to prevent dogs from escaping or fleeing into the streets? Check to see if fences are high enough to prevent doggy escapes. Are medications and cleaning chemicals stored out of paw's reach? Is there a safe, confined outdoor area for dogs, or do handlers make sure dogs are walked on leashes? Does the staff insist that all dogs wear ID tags?

- What type of exercise does the center offer? Where are dogs walked, and what are the safety procedures during these walks? For how long are dogs walked each day?
- How noisy is the center? Is there nonstop barking? Does it seem like the staff is in charge, or do dogs roam freely without supervision?
- What types of toys and equipment are provided for dogs playing in groups? Are these toys safe?
- Is clean water available in every room? What is the feeding procedure?

- Check out the credentials of the director and staff.
- What plans are in place for emergencies or for locating a veterinarian?
- Does the center require that dogs be spayed or neutered, current on their vaccinations, and on regular flea and tick maintenance programs? How do they confirm adherence to these requirements?
- How does the staff introduce new dogs to the pack of regulars? Some places like to have a staff member shadow the new dog for a day or two to ease her acceptance by the other dogs.

A Happy Doggy Day Care Client

Madison, a 50-pound, five-year-old, caramel-colored vizsla, bounds through the opened front door of Camp Happy Dog and scampers toward camp owner Deborah Nabb, who is waiting with a food treat at the check-in counter. "Sit, Madison. Okay, right paw. Good. Now left paw. Good, Madison!" says Nabb, as she delivers the food treat to Madison. Madison is one of two dozen or so regulars at Nabb's Camp Happy Dog, a Sherman Oaks, California, day care center that caters exclusively to dogs. The 3,000-square-foot, air-conditioned facility features supervised areas that permit dogs to romp and play safely.

Following Madison is her owner, Brian Kramer, a busy professional photographer. He began bringing Madison to the day care center about four years ago. Two or three days a week, depending on the demands of his day, Kramer drops off Madison and watches guilt-free as she dashes to play with Rudy, a boxer, and other regulars inside a cedarwood circular partition that features a large plastic slide, water bowls, and toys. "At first my friends thought I was spoiling my dog, but now they realize the benefits of doggy day care," says Kramer. "They've seen the improvement in Madison. She has learned obedience, some cool tricks, and gets to socialize with other friendly dogs, rather than spend the day alone at home."

Kramer describes Madison as a high-energy dog who needs a daily outlet. The two jog on weekends and occasionally hike, but Madison needs a way to unleash her pent-up vigor during weekdays. The solution: doggy day care. "I've found that it is cheaper to send Madison to day care than to replace the expensive shoes or items in my house that she would destroy from being bored and home alone all day," says Kramer. "Day cares let dogs be dogs in a healthy, safe way. When Madison comes home from day care, she sleeps soundly throughout the night."

Some day care centers, like Nabb's, bill themselves as one-stop-shopping places by offering full grooming, bathing, and dog training services, plus an array of pet foods and supplies. Others, such as Rebecca Bisgyer's Dog-Ma Day Care for Dogs, in Washington, D.C., prefer to focus on providing day care services minus the retail products.

Make sure that the center does temperament tests on dogs and properly segregates highly submissive or fearful dogs from highly confident, dominant dogs.

- How do the staff members interact with your dog? Do they show genuine affection and ask specific questions about your dog's health and behaviors?
- Will the center staff allow you to do a trial run? Schedule your dog to spend one day at the center. When you come to pick her up at the end of the day, notice how your dog behaves. Does she seem happy and relaxed or anxious and tense? Does she easily go up to members of the staff or cower and back away from them?
- Does the center offer auxiliary services such as dog food supplies, grooming, and training classes? Some places offer volume discounts or special trial rates. Grooming and bathing often cost extra.
- Are the rates reasonable? Depending on the location in the country and the type of services, doggy day care rates range from $15 to $35 per day.
- Will the center give you a list of references of clients for you to contact on your own?
- Does the center offer pickup and drop-off services?
- What are the center's hours of operation?

Dog Kennels and Hotels

If you need to travel for work or vacation and must leave your dog behind, consider the new generation of dog kennels that are more hotel-like in their amenities. Top-notch boarding places provide 24-hour attendants, private suites, scheduled playtimes, discounts for two or more guests, and plenty of toys, treats, and social activities. They also honor your dog's dietary needs. Instead of being locked inside a metal cage or a concrete run, dogs are housed in a cozy kennel that features plenty of windows for viewing ongoing activities and have safe access to the indoors and outdoors. The kennels often feature doggy beds and other pieces of furniture to mimic a home setting. Don't laugh, but some even provide radios and televisions for their canine clientele.

Reputable boarding places welcome a get-acquainted visit and an inspection of their facilities. Many of the points addressed in the checklist for doggy day cares can be applied here. Good boarding places fill up quickly, so you will need to book your dog's reservation in advance.

Don't forget to check on the kennel's hours of operation. Ideally, you want a place that's open on Sundays so you can pick up your dog upon returning from a trip. Too often, dog owners are filled with guilt because they can't be reunited with their dogs until Monday evening after their first day back to work.

Let your dog, however, be the final test of the kennel. If she bounds back into the place with a wagging tail and a happy grin, chances are that she had a good experience there. But if your dog enters the facility and starts to whine and backpedal, consider other kennels or other options for caring for your dog during your absence.

Dog Camps

Sometimes you deserve fun getaways with your dog. That's where people such as Lonnie Olson can step in and be your ally. Olson, a professional dog trainer, operates Dog Scouts of America camp in St. Helen, Michigan. Yep, you guessed it—the canine version of camps for Boy Scouts and Girl Scouts—an ideal place for dogs and people to have fun together.

Each summer and fall, Olson hosts activity-filled fun camps in a scenic wooded area where dogs learn to paint paw-pleasing pictures, play water games, and enjoy hiking trails with their owners. And, yes, dogs even earn merit badges at this camp, where the ultimate goal is to strengthen the people-pet bond and teach interactive games.

The camp offers a special time for the entire family to break away from the routine and enjoy an entertaining time with their dogs. Dogs of all sizes, shapes, and ages (beyond eight months) are welcome. By the end of camp, everyone is chanting the Dog Scout motto, "Let us learn new things that we may become more helpful."

In selecting a camp where you can spend a few days or a week with your dog, we recommend those where the atmosphere is noncompetitive and the emphasis is on fun. There are a lot of dog camps offering a variety of themes and purposes.

In Friendsville, Pennsylvania, the Ready for Prime Time Dog Performance Camp is a mecca for stardom-seeking dogs. Professional dog trainers Laurie and Mike Williams host this camp each fall. For four

A Happy Camper

Each June, Maggie and Jim Ouillette reserve five vacation days from their jobs, pack their three dogs into their car, and drive four hours to Dog Scouts of America camp. "What we like is that at camp, dogs are welcomed everywhere you go," says Maggie, a registered nurse from Whitmore Lake, Michigan. Her husband works as an employee at a local gas company. "Our dogs, Teaser, Sarah, and Molly, can approach people and get petted or receive treats. It's like a doggy paradise."

Teaser is a fun-loving golden retriever; Sarah is a task-oriented Border collie, and Molly is a scent-led beagle mix. This canine trio has earned merit badges for hiking, swimming, and other activities. At camp, they also get the chance to learn new tricks at their Tricks 101 class, plus show off ones they've mastered to others. "We love learning new things with our dogs," says Maggie. "We couldn't think of a better way to spend our summer vacations than at camp with our dogs."

days, dogs learn how to incorporate obedience, agility, canine freestyle, flyball, water work, and other activities into marketable showbiz skills. Trainers from the nation's top animal talent agencies travel to this camp to help owners bring out their dogs' hidden acting talents. "We teach skills that a dog must be able to do to land a role, such as walking up a ramp into a truck, or spinning inward, or maintaining eye contact with you at all times, despite the distractions on the movie set," explains Laurie Williams. Once a dog masters some crowd-pleasing tricks at the camp, she needs to practice them in public places to hone her skills and sharpen her focus.

Is There a Veterinarian in the House?

Is your dog overdue for her distemper or rabies vaccinations? Do you find yourself booking appointments with your veterinarian only to have to cancel them because of work demands? Does your dog turn into a puddle of panic the minute she steps into a veterinary clinic? The solution: rely on a veterinarian willing to make house calls. No more episodes of your anxious dog urinating in your car, vomiting, or becoming filled with stress as you pull into the parking space at the veterinary clinic. No more missing valuable work time sitting in a waiting room filled with barking dogs, hissing cats, and screaming children. With your dog on her home turf, a veterinarian is able to get a complete picture of her environment, which often helps the doctor diagnose a medical condition or unwanted behavior. Let's run down the pluses of house-call veterinarian visits:

- **Convenience:** If you own more than one pet, you don't have to struggle to load all of them into your vehicle or make multiple trips to the veterinary clinic to make sure that they all receive regular checkups. You can relax in your living room instead of struggling to keep all your leashed and caged pets calm and by your side.

- **Comfort:** A dog in her home displays far less stress than one inside a clinic. There should be less struggle and anxious wiggling.

- **Safety:** Although veterinary hospitals are conscious of hygiene, a lot of sick animals come and go. They bring viruses, bacteria, and parasites. Your dog receiving checkups at home does not run the risk of picking up a disease or getting in a scrap with another dog in the waiting room.

- **Cost:** House-call fees may be slightly higher that costs charged at clinics. House-call veterinarians offer personalized attention and must spend part of their work day on the road. They refer sick pets to appropriate veterinary hospitals and

Meet Roger Valentine, House-Call Vet

Roger Valentine, D.V.M., is always on the go. Six days a week, he drives a champagne-colored Jeep Cherokee with the license plate CATDVM1 and blends conventional care with holistic medicine for nearly five thousand dogs and cats in the Los Angeles area. He operates an animal clinic in Santa Monica but spends most of his days on the road making house calls. He capped off one long workweek by maneuvering his Jeep up the winding Canyon Road, in Beverly Hills. He stepped out of his vehicle to a chorus of friendly barks from Eva, Snoopy, and Kaiser—three large dogs owned by Susan Capano. Rather than struggle to bring all three dogs in for a veterinary exam, Capano schedules at-home appointments with Dr. Valentine to meet her dogs' medical needs.

Dr. Valentine has been making house calls for more than a decade and has no plans of stopping. "The days can be long and unpredictable, but I love making house calls," he says. "From the medical standpoint, I get to see the entire environment in which the dogs live, and that helps me pinpoint the problems better. Each visit is certainly an adventure, posing its own set of challenges."

share the patients' medical records and diagnostic test results with hospital veterinary staff.

- **Peace of mind:** If it should be necessary to euthanize your sick or senior dog, a house-call veterinarian can perform this procedure in your home with your family and other pets present to pay due respect to your departing dog.

While there are a lot of advantages to house-call veterinary practices, there are some cautions as well. If you want the house-call veterinarian to be in charge of all of your pet's needs, make sure this veterinarian has arrangements in place with full-service hospitals and emergency clinics. If your current doctor does advanced procedures, he or she is likely to have hospital privileges at one or more facilities. The same will likely be true for your house-call veterinarian. After all, you wouldn't expect your house-call veterinarian to perform orthopedic surgery in the back of a vehicle or on your kitchen table.

In some cases, dogs are more protective on their home turf, and this can be a problem for home-based health care. You also need to be aware that there will likely be increased costs associated with a veterinarian who arrives at your door. Other than that, use the same care you would to pick a regular veterinarian and hospital, and enjoy the convenience.

Finding a veterinarian who makes house calls is easier than you might imagine. Check with the American Association of House Call Veterinarians (www.athomevet.org) or the AVMA (www.avma.org) for referrals in your area. The growing popularity of this service has prompted the American Animal Hospital Association to offer an accreditation program for mobile veterinarians.

Have Clippers, Will Travel

Home delivery isn't limited to veterinarians these days. Now your dog can be bathed and have his coat clipped and shaped without having to leave your property. If only hairstylists for people would make house calls!

Certain breeds, especially poodles and cocker spaniels, require regular baths and trims. If you're pressed for time, consider hiring a professional dog groomer who makes house calls. You don't have to spend precious time packing up your dog, driving her to the salon, and picking her up later. And it's especially beneficial if you own a dog who is prone to car sickness or is fearful or shy. Some dogs can be traumatized by all the commotion inside a dog salon. Many are dropped off in the morning and must wait—often in crates—all day until their owners can pick them up after work.

These are some of the amenities a groomer uses.

Some professional dog groomers will use your shower or bathtub to clean your dog.

You can often make arrangements for the groomer to come during the day while you're at work. Your dog receives full attention from a groomer who is not distracted by interruptions (other dogs, ringing telephones, customers) common inside a salon. Some groomers can use your shower or bathtub to clean your dog. Others rely on mobile grooming vans, equipped with all the amenities needed to turn a dirty, shaggy dog into a clean, coiffed canine. These salons on wheels feature large sinks or tubs, a grooming table, heating for cool weather, air-conditioning for warm weather, and handheld blow dryers.

Expect to pay more for mobile grooming services: $10 to $15 above what you'd pay for a salon treatment at a shop. But the convenience and the reassurance of knowing your dog's grooming needs are being regularly addressed should easily outweigh paying the extra dollars.

Dog-Friendly Bosses

An often overlooked ally is your employer. Some companies are downright dog friendly and allow employees to bring dogs to work. No longer merely the domain of fire stations or junkyards, dogs are making their way into a variety of workplaces across the nation. They are becoming as common as dressing casually on Fridays and annual office picnics. In 2001, for example, about five thousand companies participated in the annual Take Your Dog to Work Day, an event created and sponsored by Pet Sitters International. Start-up companies, mom-and-pop businesses, and even corporations are putting out the welcome mat for dogs. In fact, a new trend is to expand employee benefit packages to include such dog-pleasing perks as paying for pet sitting for employees traveling on company business, veterinary pet insurance, in-house kennels, and in-office sessions with professional dog trainers.

What can canines bring to the bottom line? Business owners who allow dogs in their workplace often benefit from employee morale boosts and workers willing to stay late to finish tasks rather than dash home to tend to their dogs. Employers who long ago realized the merits of child care for their employees with children are suddenly discovering that the same principles apply for pet owners. Imagine that!

You may also inquire at work to see if your supervisor would be willing to let you work some hours from home or bring home paperwork rather than work late.

At Mercedes Medical, Inc., a medical supply company in Sarasota, Florida, Scott Gerber, vice president for sales, reports that absenteeism and turnover are low because well-mannered dogs are permitted there.

Dawn D'Angelillo, a marketing representative, accepted a position at Small Dog Electronics, Inc., in Waitsfield, Vermont, partly because of the company's pet policy. Every day she heads for work accompanied by Libby, her yellow Labrador retriever. "Having Libby here takes the stress out of work, and I find that I get a lot more work done," says D'Angelillo.

John Reddington, D.V.M., Ph.D., owner of DiaXotics, in Wilton, Connecticut, believes in reimbursing employees for pet-sitting services when they must travel on company business and permitting pet bereavement days with pay. He says it's simply good business practice. "Dogs get the chance to be socialized, and companies benefit by getting top-quality people who are compassionate," says Dr. Reddington.

Allowing dogs in the workplace takes work—and rules are necessary. Many companies issue the Three

Some companies allow you to bring your dog to work.

Many employees feel that having their dog by their side takes the stress out of work.

Ps rule: if a dog makes three pees (or poops) in inappropriate places, the dog loses office privileges. Often, common areas such as conference rooms, cafeterias, break rooms, and restrooms are off-limits to dogs out of respect for employees who may have allergies to or are afraid of dogs or who simply do not enjoy them. Dogs need to obey basic commands such as *down* and *stay* and must be quiet so employees can do their jobs. Dogs must be current on their vaccinations and be well groomed and flea-free. Employees who bring dogs to work must pack more than a briefcase. They need to bring doggy essentials: a 6-foot leash, buckle collar, water bowl, some poop-scooping bags, food treats, chew toys, toys that don't squeak, and in some cases baby gates to keep the dogs out of certain areas of the office. Some company hand-books even include doggy rules, speci-fying that dogs can't be destructive or disruptive.

If your company doesn't let you take your dog to work, ask if you can work from home some of the time.

Dogs in the workplace do run the risk of becoming too chubby if well-meaning employees constantly dole out treats to them. We encourage dog owners to politely set treat-feeding guidelines for coworkers to keep their dogs healthy.

If your company doesn't allow employees to bring pets to work daily, maybe you can encourage the company to participate in the annual Take Your Dog to Work Day. You can request an Action Packet at www.petsit.com. "Companies spend millions of dollars trying to figure out ways to lessen stress and increase productivity among their workers," says Patti Moran, founder of Pet Sitters International. "We've introduced a secret weapon that can do all this with a lick on the face."

CHAPTER 6

* * * * * * * * * *

HOW TO OWN A DOG AND STILL HAVE A SOCIAL LIFE

* * * * * * * * * *

Does it ever feel like you're the one who is tethered to the end of a long leash? Since you've become a dog owner, does it seem as if your social life has taken a nosedive? Do you find yourself renting videos rather than going to first-run movies at theaters? Do you reluctantly turn down coworkers' spur-of-the-moment invitations to happy hour? Or wish you could clone yourself so you could attend you son's soccer match and your dog's obedience class—both at the same time? Do you cut short a Saturday outing so that you can rush home to let your dog out for a bathroom break? Do you feel confined by having a dog waiting at home for your return? It doesn't have to be this way. You can own a dog and be a good parent and maintain a social life—without a lick of guilt or an ounce of resentment. No need to feel torn between making a living and making your home livable for your stay-behind dog.

Need some encouragement? First, consider this: Dogs don't feel guilt. They're not sitting at home on

Your dog should add to your enjoyment of life.

your couch, spewing out hair, and fretting over the "what ifs" or the "should haves" in life. They are not repentant for the shoe they "killed" and chewed two days ago, nor are they worrying whether their food bowl will be filled two days from now. We could actually learn a lot about how to deal with life from our canine companions. In many ways, they seem to take a Zen-like approach to life because they live in the moment, not in the past or the future.

Second, remember that you're not alone. Millions of dog owners must work for a living. Like the rest of the dog-owning population, you deserve to unwind from a long day by spending after-work hours with your friends. It is unrealistic for you to expect to be home 24 hours a day. Who would want that?

Third, dogs don't ask for much, and they expect even less. You can be a good dog parent by providing your dog with the essentials while you're away: a comfy bed, fresh water, a few favorite toys, some treats, and a couple of nice viewing areas to watch the action in the neighborhood.

In this chapter we will help you melt away that guilt glacier by introducing you to a few dog lovers who offer savvy strategies and solutions that help put your mind at ease when you're out and about without your dog. We will also show you how owning a dog can actually improve your social life and possibly lead to true romance or rekindle new love in your current relationship. Remember that this is not a book about making you feel guilty about caring for your canine companion. We're here to help you make the most of the situation; we're not here to have you give up all your social time to spend caring for a dog. Owning a dog should add to your enjoyment of life, not detract from it.

Enlisting the Help of Dog-Loving Kids

If you have children, your dog can participate in teaching them life lessons and responsibilities. Imagine the important lessons learned when we teach our children to care for and respect pets in our households. When pets have veterinary needs, we take care of them. When we have to be away from home, we make plans to ensure their continued care. When children have priority chores that involve caring for the family dog, the kids realize that they can't just postpone these duties when something more exciting comes along. There is a living, breathing creature at home depending on them. When you assign your child some of the dog-care responsibility, everyone wins. You'll have more time (guilt-free) for other things, the child learns important life lessons, and the dog has his needs met by an enthusiastic playmate. Generally, by age 7, children can be given some dog-caring duties such as keeping the

By giving your child some of the dog-care responsibility, he will learn important life lessons.

water bowl filled with fresh water. Parents need to use their judgments on what their children can do based on their maturity levels.

There are other valuable lessons that can be learned by caring for living things. Studies have shown that men who own dogs make better fathers, likely because they appreciate the needs of dependents, regardless of species. There is also enough

Dog-loving kids will jump at the chance to help you care for your dog.

troubling evidence that children who treat animals cruelly often grow up to commit violent crimes against people. When children see their household dogs treated as a nuisance or as a disposable novelty, imagine what negative behaviors they are learning. Conversely, many great dog owners were children when they learned how to be compassionate and caring toward canines.

If you don't have children to assign duties to, look for neighbor kids who want to care for a dog but don't have one. Even if you can't hire a child, you still have several options to keep your social life manageable. And if you are a couple without children, a dog may help you decide if you're ready to be parents. After all, if between the two of you, you can't find time to walk the dog, it's best not to run out quite yet to start decorating the nursery.

Getting Help from Neighbors and Pet Sitters

Let's start with the story of Squirt. For 10 years, this spirited cairn terrier has been Anne Egan's faithful friend. Squirt has been with Egan through key life transitions: new boyfriends, new jobs, and new homes. Egan, a food editor for a national publishing company, enjoys coming home from work and taking Squirt out for a predinner walk through her Allentown, Pennsylvania, neighborhood. Halfway through the walk on the tree-lined sidewalks, Squirt insists on walking herself, proudly holding the end of the leather leash in her mouth until she marches up to the front door of their Tudor-style house. It's a ritual they both enjoy.

But sometimes this early evening routine gets interrupted when Egan accepts after-work drink invitations, needs to put in a 12-hour workday, or must attend an out-of-town conference. Yet, not once in 10 years has Egan boarded Squirt at a kennel—not a single time. What's her secret? Egan has relied on helpful neighbors and trustworthy pet sitters to care for Squirt when she's away.

When Egan lived in New Jersey, she and a neighbor exchanged house keys and provided dog-watching services for each other. The neighbor owned a

Your dogs will appreciate having a neighbor let them out when you have to work late.

Yorkshire terrier named Gumby, a dog Squirt enjoyed sharing walks with. A cooperative you-walk-my-dog-I'll-walk-yours alliance was formed.

When Egan relocated to Allentown a few years ago, she adopted a new puppy, Simba, a Japanese chin-shih tzu mix. Egan consulted her dogs' new veterinarian about reputable dog sitters. Her veterinarian put her in touch with a licensed and bonded professional pet sitter who lived only fifteen minutes from Egan's home. "I couldn't live without her—whether I'm coming home late from work or need to be gone for a few days on business, she comes to my house and walks and feeds Squirt and Simba," says Egan. "To me, she is worth every penny."

On those rare occasions when Egan needs to work late and the pet sitter is unavailable, Egan comes home expecting to clean up a couple of puddles on her floor. She knows not to blame or punish her dogs. Instead, she comes in the door, takes them out for a walk, returns inside, and matter-of-factly cleans up the messes without any sighing or angriness in her voice. "That's why cleaning products were invented," she declares.

Some dogs can be trained to be catlike by learning to use litters created especially for indoor dogs. Most of these litter kits contain nontoxic pellet-formed litter made from recyclable paper, a litter pan, and a step-by-step instruction manual. They are primarily designed for puppies and dogs up to 35 pounds, but larger dogs can use them as backup bathrooms in case their owners are unable to come home at the usual time.

Many Options Available for Cocoa

In Atlantis, Florida, Susan Baker shares her three-bedroom home in a private golf community with Cocoa, a highly intelligent three-year-old black standard poodle. When time permits, Baker, a national newspaper editor, tries to come home on her lunch hour to walk Cocoa. But during most weekdays, Cocoa lounges inside a spacious crate situated in Baker's tiled dining room. Inside the crate are a water bowl, a comfy blanket, and a handful of treats. "She is much calmer inside her crate than roaming free in the house alone," says Baker. "She gets too anxious having the whole house to herself when I'm gone. She knows that her crate is her home, her safe place."

If Baker needs to stay late at work or wants to fly to see her parents, who live in northwest Indiana, she has several backup plans to care for Cocoa. If she realizes she will be coming home late, she contacts a neighbor who lives two doors down. This neighbor, a retiree, owns Peppy, a male poodle. The four met a few times during early evening walks. Baker noticed how caring her neighbor is toward Peppy. The neighbor noticed that Baker sometimes arrives home late after work. "She offered to walk and feed Cocoa for me," says Baker. "She knows what it is like to own a poodle. The two dogs get along great, and when she offered again, I said yes. She gives me peace of mind. She won't accept any money, but I do treat her to dinners occasionally as my way of saying thanks."

When Baker has to travel, she sends Cocoa to stay with her dog groomer, who owns a miniature poodle named Holly. Cocoa gets to socialize with a pet-friendly family and play with a miniversion of herself. Baker's third option is boarding Cocoa at her veterinarian's clinic. Cocoa receives a warm reception from the staff each time she arrives. She stays in a homelike kennel and gets plenty of exercise and attention while Baker is away. "I feel better knowing that she is at the veterinary clinic. If there would be a medical crisis, she would be able to get immediate attention," says Baker.

House Hunting with Max in Mind

On the West Coast, family therapist and animal behavior consultant Larry Lachman has honed many options to care for Max, his seven-year-old flat-coated retriever. As much as possible, Max rides with Dr. Lachman when he needs to make short trips to the bank, fast-food restaurant, or grocery store. Dr. Lachman always parks in the shade, opens the tinted windows of his Chevy Tahoe a couple of inches, and makes sure that Max has fresh water, some chew toys, and a handful of biscuits. "I don't leave him for long periods, but by giving Max the biscuits each time I leave the car, he has learned to associate my leaving with something positive," explains Dr. Lachman.

When he moved to Carmel, California, a couple of years ago, Dr. Lachman purposely searched for a rental home with Max in mind. He selected a home within ten minutes of a dog park. During the day, Max has access to the backyard through a doggy door in the living room. An 8-foot-high fence that borders the backyard gives Dr. Lachman peace of mind in knowing that Max is safe.

Caring for Max

When Dr. Lachman needs to travel for a day or longer, he selects these Max-caring options in order:

- ✔ He hires a professional pet sitter/dog walker to stay in his home with Max.
- ✔ He brings Max with him when he stays overnight in the homes of friends or family members who know—and adore—this body-wiggling, happy-go-lucky dog.
- ✔ As a last resort, he sends Max to a kennel where dogs are pampered in style.

"As much as possible, I try to leave Max at home, in his own environment, where he feels the most comfortable. I refer to the pet sitter who stays with Max as his live-in nanny," says Dr. Lachman.

Finding More Time for Yourself by Adopting a Dog

New dog owner Lori Davis, of Allentown, Pennsylvania, has found that the added responsibility of caring for a dog works to her advantage. Before she adopted Lacey, a shy three-year-old sheltie, this single magazine researcher found it extremely difficult to decline social invitations, even those spur-of-the-moment ones. "Being single, it seemed like I had no excuse to say no to drinks after work," says Davis. "There were weeks when I would be out every night, and after a while, that can get tiring—and, frankly, expensive."

Within months after buying her first home, Davis felt ready to own a dog. Rather than adopt a puppy, she realized that her lifestyle was better suited to

adopting an older dog who didn't need her to spend time house-training. Friends told her about a dog rescue organization, where she got matched up with Lacey, whose elderly owner had died.

Davis wanted the companionship of a furry friend but also realized that she needed to add some structure and responsibility to her life. In her case, Davis was actually looking for an acceptable excuse to curtail her social life a bit. Life with Lacey has given her that and more. Davis has discovered that she is more efficient with her time at work so she can get home at a decent hour. She is also learning how to be more selective about accepting social invitations both after work and on weekends. "Now I can use the excuse that I have to get home to feed and walk my dog," says Davis. "And if I'm on a date that doesn't really seem to be working out, I can politely excuse myself early by saying that I need to get home to my dog. No longer am I always going to be available every time the phone rings. And I enjoy spending time at home with Lacey. She is helping me bring balance to my life."

A dog can redirect your social priorities. Instead of spending after-work hours at bars or Saturday nights at the movies, you can find friends with similar interests—thanks to your dog.

Looking for Love in All the Doggy Places

Love-seekers turned off by singles bars, blind dates, and church socials are finding soul mates by unleashing the matchmaking powers of their canine companions. They are meeting and mingling at dog parks, sharing sweet nothings through Internet chat rooms that cater to pet lovers, posting pet-friendly classified ads, and becoming friendly rivals at dog agility and breed shows.

Are dogs the ultimate answer to finding more than puppy love? Possibly, say relationship therapists and animal behaviorists. Finding Mr. or Ms. Right could be a bark away. "Let's face it, it's a grab bag at a bar when trying to find someone who has at least one hobby in common with you," said Alan Beck, Sc.D., a professor at Purdue University's School of Veterinary Medicine, in West Lafayette, Indiana, and coauthor of *Between Pets and People: The Importance of Animal Companionship.* "Then you meet someone who has a friendly dog on a leash," he continues. "Your perception is that this is a caring, responsible person who values what you value. Dogs make terrific icebreakers and allow you to feel comfortable enough to approach a person and speak with them."

Credit the need to walk her dog and his need to visit a chiropractor for bringing Debra and John DeNicola together on a street in busy New York City. John normally would never be on Grove Street, where Debra's apartment is, but he was making the walk to be treated by a chiropractor whose office was down the block. When John first spotted Debra taking her German shepherd-chow chow mix, Skat , out for a walk, he was smitten. Trying his best to slow his pace as Skat constantly stopped to sniff, John finally stopped himself, turned around, and blurted out to Debra, "Are you married or going out with anybody?" Debra overlooked John's stumbling first line and focused on Skat's body cues. "Normally, Skat is

pulling on the leash, letting me know he wants to go, but he was very relaxed around John and sat down while we talked for a very long time. I took that as a good sign," said Debra, who married John eight years ago. Today they share their Grove Street apartment with their young son, Jake, and Skat.

Dogs served as canine cupids for Elizabeth and Tommy Allen of New York City, and Kista and Robert Icard of San Francisco. If not for their dogs playing tail-wagging matchmakers, they might never have met, dated, and exchanged wedding vows. "When we met, it was instant magnetism," said Elizabeth Allen, a designer of evening and bridal wear, who married Tommy, a record producer/musician. The two met on a freezing cold day. Elizabeth was walking her bulldog, Dozer, and Tommy was walking his golden retriever puppy, Pope. The two dogs started playing on the sidewalk as Elizabeth and Tommy made eye contact. "The minute we started talking to each other, we knew we were going to get married," says Elizabeth Allen.

Robert Icard won Kista's heart six years ago when he gave her a black Labrador puppy named Layla as a Valentine's Day gift. Rarely a day apart since then, they married two years ago. The outdoor ceremony was highlighted by Layla, decked out in a collar of faux pearls, trotting down the aisle as ring bearer. Invitees included 30 people, 4 dogs, 2 cats, and an aquarium of fish. "Both of us are so attached to animals that we wanted them to share in our ceremony. The only requirement was that the dogs had to be on leashes," said Kista, who, with Robert, works at the San Francisco Society for the Prevention of Cruelty to Animals (SPCA) shelter.

These days, dog parks serve as ideal places for singles to meet and talk. Typically there is a brief silence, followed by some remark about the other person's dog, and then the conversation and interaction begin. Being social pack animals, dogs help enhance people's social skills as well.

For pet owners not inclined to go to dog parks, there is always the Internet. Susan Kordich of Brooklyn, New York, cofounded Pet Lovers Unite, a Web site dedicated to pet owners looking for human companionship. "We found that people were fed up with the traditional methods of finding mates," she said. "Being on-line, you can talk with people not only in your hometown but across the United States and in other countries as well. We have three hundred members, and the list keeps growing every day."

Sometimes the love of a dog can reignite the love shared by a husband and wife who have been married for many years. Tev and Scott Brannon of Plano, Texas, never squabbled much during their 25 years of marriage, but about 10 years ago, they began spending weekends apart. Scott, who works for a major hotel chain, chased the challenge of an 18-hole golf course. Tev flocked to pedigree dog shows to admire the poise and posture of champion canines. Then a friend told Tev about a new type of dog competition: agility training, where pedigrees and mutts are welcome to compete in timed events that test their abilities to make sharp turns, leap over barriers, walk on wobbly surfaces, and duck in

and out of tunnels. Owners race in stride with their dogs and give them encouragement and instruction.

Tev took her two shelties, Amber and Spree, one weekend to witness a local competition. Intrigued, she kept going back, first as an observer and then as a participant. One weekend she coaxed her husband into forgoing golf and joining her. That was eight years ago. Now the Brannons and their dogs drive around the country on weekends to compete in agility contests. "We discovered this common interest," said Tev. "Our marriage was never in trouble, but I do believe that our dogs and the agility competitions have helped enhance our marriage. This is something we definitely both enjoy."

The bottom line is that dogs do not need to be viewed as time-stealers. As the above examples illustrate, you, too, can enjoy a full social life and kiss those guilt-ridden feelings goodbye.

Agility competitions are a fun thing for you and your dog to do together.

CHAPTER 7

★ ★ ★ ★ ★ ★ ★ ★ ★ ★

GETTING ACTIVE WITH YOUR DOG

★ ★ ★ ★ ★ ★ ★ ★ ★

On most weekends, from Boston to San Diego, you can find dogs leaping for Frisbees, dancing the cha-cha, and ushering cattle—all in the name of sport. In Los Alamitos, California, stubby-legged dachshunds duel in 50-yard dashes to raise money for local animal shelters. In Chicago, teams of leaping Labradors lunge for tennis balls in timed relay events. In Coltsneck, New Jersey, purebred borzois make hairpin turns at full stride to reach the often just-out-of-reach plastic lure.

Today's generation of athletic dogs are leaping off couches and into dozens of sports venues. Mixed breeds mingle with pedigreed dogs in Frisbee and flyball. Gray-muzzled tail-waggers prove you can teach old dogs new tricks—or at least new dance steps—in canine musical freestyle, which is quickly growing in popularity. Events take place in dance halls, gymnasiums, cattle arenas, tree-lined woods, and sprawling meadows.

While dogs have their day in the ever-expanding sporting world, people discover the fun and thrill of teaming up with their canine companions and meeting people with similar interests. Engaging in active fun reduces stress for both dog and owner, and it certainly strengthens the human-animal companion bond. Many of today's sports promote companionship and collaboration above competition. Organized sporting events give dogs an outlet for pent-up energy. Although some participants receive special recognition, all come away winners. "People participating in performance events are willing to

Many dogs like to play Frisbee.

spend time with their dogs and develop positive relationships," said Ken Tatsch, executive director of the United States Dog Agility Association in Richardson, Texas. "They become more responsible dog owners, and their dogs become better behaved."

Let's take a look at some organized activities that you can share with your dog. These aren't the only human-canine activities out there by a long shot, but they are among the most popular.

Agility

Dog agility involves you, your off-lead dog, an obstacle course, and a timer. You've probably seen agility events on television; they are extremely exciting. Some of the obstacles used in a course include pipe tunnels, weave poles, A-frames, hoop jumps, and seesaws. The obstacles are arranged in various course configurations, which are different from trial to trial, that offer challenges appropriate to the class and experience level of the dogs competing. This keeps each new competition exciting for both dog and handler.

Your job, as handler, is to direct your dog around the course in a predetermined sequence, using signals only; you are not allowed to physically touch your dog or the equipment while she is actively competing. You can give as many commands and signals as you want, but don't touch or you'll be disqualified. Don't worry that your dog may be too small to make a big jump; dogs compete only against other dogs of similar height. As you and your canine companion get better and better, you can enter advanced competitions with tougher courses. It really doesn't matter if you win or lose— just competing with your pooch in a beginning competition is rewarding enough.

Even smaller dogs can compete in agility competitions.

Engaging in active fun strengthens the human-animal companion bond.

Earthdog Trials

You may not hear this in polite company, but many terriers and dachshunds were bred to flush out vermin. Hopefully there is no need for this in your home. These dogs have an instinctive drive to enter burrows and dens in search of vermin, and this instinct is utilized in earthdog trials. The object is for a dog to approach a constructed tunnel and follow a scent into the tunnel to a quarry (typically a caged rat, who is not physically harmed in the process) within a specified time period. Then the dog is required to "work" the quarry for a set time period by barking, pawing, digging, and generally being a nuisance to the rat. The big downside to this sport is that most of the action happens underground, but it's always nice to witness a skill that was bred into a dog.

Flyball

If you are into team sports, fast-action flyball may be just the activity for you. You might not think so, but this is a sport for just about any breed of dog, not just the natural sprinters. Even basset hounds have competed and earned respect. Basically, flyball is a relay race involving four dogs, hurdles, and a spring-loaded box that shoots out tennis balls. What could be better than that?

The first dog races down the 51-foot course, jumping the four hurdles, then reaches the spring-loaded box at which time a dog must press a lever to activate the launch of a tennis ball. She catches the tennis ball and clears the four hurdles on the way back to the starting line. Then the next dog on the team starts. You might not think it much of a sport, but don't blink or you'll miss a match. Most are completed in less than 30 seconds, and points are awarded to team members based on the team's time. Twenty points entitles you to refer to your dog as a flyball dog (FD), while thirty thousand points are required to become a Flyball Grand Champion (FGDCh). May the force—and flying tennis ball—be with you!

Flying Disc Events

There are a variety of competitions that involve throwing discs, such as Frisbees, for dogs to catch and retrieve. In the catch-and-retrieve class, typically the owner throws a disc, judges measure the distance from the throw to the dog's catch, and scores are given based on the number of completed catches in a given time period, with the distance being factored in. A separate class is freestyle, sometimes referred to as free flight, which is typically a timed routine performed to music. It's a choreographed event, featuring tricks, throws, and spectacular catches. You can reach professional status in these events, but if you want to maintain your amateur status, participate in events only at local parks. With the right canine partner, flying disc events can be a lot of fun.

Flying disc events are fun for both you and your dog.

Musical Freestyle

This blend of dance and obedience work demonstrates the dog's ability not only to move fluidly with the music but also to respond seamlessly with a human dance partner. Every performance is different, as it involves unique music, choreography, and dog-human dynamic. Don't worry too much if you have two left feet—so does your canine dancing partner. The judges are looking for the dog to be moving to the beat and to be responding to his or her human partner.

This event is gaining in popularity with each passing year, and a number of international organizations sanction matches. If you have artistic flair and share this quality with your dog, you just might have a team sport that meets both of your needs. Bring on the Chihuahua cha-cha or the terrier tango!

Obedience Trials

While not as fast-paced as some of the other activities mentioned, obedience trials have been around for more than 50 years and are sanctioned by a variety of breed clubs. In the novice class, points are given for successful ability to heel on a leash, perform a walking figure eight, stand for examination, do a long sit, and do a long down. By the time your dog advances to the utility class, she performs signal exercises, scent discrimination, and directed jumping. Tracking competition is also part of obedience. As you might expect from the name, the competition identifies those animals who best obey the commands of their handler.

Showing

Showing is the quintessential dog event, involving beautiful dogs and a lot of showmanship. While the big shows such as Westminster and Crufts garner all the media attention, there are also a lot of shows held locally all across the country. Whether you want to show your dog in obedience, conformation, hunting, agility, herding, or any of the many other events, in most cases you need a registered pedigreed dog to compete. There are also conformation shows available for mutts and dogs without papers, but for the most part this is about genes and scenes—the ancestry of the dog and how closely the dog matches the breed standard, that image of perfection for the individual breed.

Even if your pup doesn't have the accepted aristocratic air for the show ring, there's always obedience or agility to show off your dog's other talents.

If all this seems a little bit obsessive to you, remember that many groups sponsor fun matches at local

---

Showing Tips

Here are some tips if you intend to show your purebred dog in conformation:

✔ Don't neuter or spay your dog. Altering is frowned upon in this event, which helps determine which dogs should be bred to perpetuate the best aspects of the breed. (Neutering is permitted in performance events.)

✔ Make sure you have registration papers for your dog—these events are not for dogs who can't prove their pedigree.

✔ While we strongly recommend training, don't teach your conformation dog the *sit* command. Sitting in the show ring or during the examination is a big no-no in conformation.

---

events, with awards such as most photogenic, most congenial, and best kisser that might be more to your liking. In the world of dog shows, there's something for everyone.

Skijoring

If you're a winter sports enthusiast and have a large, furry, snow-loving dog, skijoring may be for you. All it takes are some cross-country skis, a good attitude, and a big dog who loves to run in the snow and pull you in tow. *Skijor* is actually a Norwegian word meaning ski driving. You put on your skis, hook up Pookie in a harness, and use her like the draft animal she always wanted to be. Of course, you're not really using Pookie to pull you. You are enjoyably cross-country skiing, and your dog partner is simply using her natural pulling instincts in front of you.

You'll need a properly fitted harness for the dog, a tether line with a bungee section, a waist belt or climbing harness for yourself, a pack to carry gear (including treats and water for both of you), and some bags to collect any poop that happens to get on the trails. Some dogs are naturally better for "pulling" sports, and some others are well adapted to the cold and snow, but if you have a Chihuahua or an Italian greyhound, better to stick to the chalets and a couch by the fire. Most skijoring dogs weigh 60 pounds or more and can comfortably run in the snow for hours. It's not for everyone, but it may just be right for the two of you!

Those who like a little extra challenge to their skijoring can use a pulk—a small sled that is loaded with gear and pulled by a dog or dogs to handicap exceptionally fast dogs or light, strong skiers. The skier is tethered to the pulk and follows it.

CHAPTER 8

* * * * * * * * *

LANDLORDS AND OTHER LIVING ARRANGEMENTS

* * * * * * * * *

You've landed the ideal job—but it's 1,200 miles away. You have three weeks to uproot your family, hire movers, and find a new place to live. You scan rental magazines, newspaper classifieds, and Web sites and then spot this ad: "For rent: 3 bedroom, 2 bath, spacious living area, fireplace, fenced backyard, quiet neighborhood, nice schools. . ." It sounds perfect—until you read the final three words: "Sorry, no pets." Your worried eyes cast a glance at the five-year-old sweet, well-mannered beagle you've had since she was a puppy. How can you possibly find a place that accepts pets?

Finding an apartment that accepts pets is a win-win situation.

Fortunately, efforts are under way to convert no-pets landlords into pet-welcoming landlords. The HSUS is leading a national campaign aimed at enlightening landlords on the values of having dog owners as tenants. Local animal organizations have joined this cause. Across the country, even in densely populated areas such as Boston, San Francisco, and Washington, D.C., more apartments are opening their doors to renters with pets. "I'm optimistic that through our efforts and the efforts of responsible pet owners more landlords will see the benefits of having pets-welcome policies," said Nancy Peterson, who is in charge of the HSUS Rent with Pets campaign. "One of the top reasons why animals are brought to shelters is because people moved and can't find a place to accept their pets. Too many dogs and cats are needlessly euthanized."

Making It a Win-Win Situation for Landlords and Tenants

Nearly one of every two renters in the United States has pets, according to a recent study by the AVMA. Even more renters would have pets if their rental properties permitted them. Animal humane groups are actively working with landlords to help them rent to responsible pet owners. They are showing how they can permit pets and maintain quality.

Why does a pets-allowed policy make sense? Let us count the ways. Landlords can choose from a larger pool of prospective renters by including those who own pets. Allowing pets may also increase the

Some apartment complexes only allow dogs up to a certain weight.

average length of occupancy. Once pet owners find a housing property or community that welcomes their pets, they are likely to rent for a longer period of time than residents who do not own pets. Pet owners grateful to find a dog-welcome place are often model residents who keep their living areas neat and clean. Finally, it's good public relations for an apartment complex to be "propets." Research has proven time and again the rewards of pet ownership to people. Pets help most of us live happier and healthier lives.

HSUS Recommendations for Apartment Owners and Managers

✓ Limit the number of pets per dwelling to ensure the renter can provide responsible care.

✓ Insist that all cats, dogs, and rabbits be neutered or spayed by age six months, and require written proof of sterilization.

✓ Require that dogs and cats be licensed and up to date on vaccinations and medical checkups.

✓ Mandate that dogs and cats wear collars with ID tags at all times.

✓ Provide instruction for proper disposal of pets' waste.

✓ Evaluate prospective tenants and pets on an individual basis. Base a decision on a pet's good behavior, not on the size or breed.

✓ Require an additional deposit to cover any damage caused by pets.

✓ Alert current residents to inform you if they intend to acquire a pet before bringing one to the development.

✓ Spell out in writing fines or lease terminations for pet owners who violate written guidelines.

PROVIDE WRITTEN PET POLICIES

Having policies in place can save landlords time and money because they no longer have to police their premises and take legal action against tenants who illegally sneak in pets. By having a written pet policy in place, apartment owners can gain better control and legally enforce what types of pets are allowed. The landlords can also ensure greater safety for all tenants by requiring that pets keep current on their vaccinations, be leashed outdoors, wear identification tags, and exhibit nonaggressive behavior.

Members of the National Multi Housing Council, based in Washington, D.C., represent the largest rental property companies in the country. Currently, this association does not have a pet policy yet, but more are admitting pets into their complexes. Jay Harris, vice president of property management, says it's good business these days to be pet friendly in the apartment industry. He says apartment complexes are better able to build a sense of community by encouraging good renters to stay.

Well-behaved dogs are permitted to reside at the apartments associated with the 16 Home Properties complexes in the Rochester, New York, area. Officials added a strict pet clause to the lease that puts responsibility in the hands of the dog owners. For example, owners who do not pick up after their dogs on bathroom outings are fined. But Home Properties is lenient when it comes to the size of the dog: it's behavior, not size, that matters most. That's good news for Hannah, a 120-pound mellow Newfoundland who shares an apartment with owners

Many apartment complexes find it to be good business to allow pets.

landlords about flea infestation. The solution: educate the landlords. Hawaiian HSUS officials successfully developed a checklist with landlords in Maui and alerted them about the new and highly effective flea control treatments available today. The Hawaiian HSUS also publishes a quarterly newsletter for property managers that discusses responsible pet ownership issues, explains animal control laws, and demonstrates the importance of the bond between people and their pets.

Contact Local Animal Shelters for Housing Help

San Francisco and New York City are high-rent, in-demand metropolitan areas. The Humane Society of Rochester and Monroe County at Lollypop Farm, in Fairport, New York, and the San Francisco SPCA do a lot of the legwork for pet-owning rental seekers in these two areas. Both groups maintain updated data-bases of pet-friendly rentals. In addition, they provide brochures on pet services, such as pet parenting classes, pet behavior counseling, and health clinics that property managers can distribute to their tenants.

Jennifer Novarr and her husband, Walter Silbert.

In Long Beach, California, managers of the 83-unit Pine Terrace apartments recently amended their pet policy to allow dogs who weigh up to 50 pounds. The previous policy limited acceptance to dogs weighing less than 25 pounds. Officials at Pine Terrace say they find that renters with dogs tend to keep their apartments in top condition and tend to stay longer than those without pets.

Let's look at a few more success stories, starting in Hawaii. For years, this island state's renting community was pet unfriendly because of concerns by

Several states, including California, now permit seniors and disabled persons living in state-subsidized housing to keep pets under certain conditions; officials can determine the number of pets allowed and the size of the pets. This legal avenue helps keep pets together with their owners. In the greater Boston area, the Massachusetts SPCA helped pass a similar law and is working to permit pets for all people living in public housing.

Helpful Tips for a Smooth Move

✓ Recognize that your dog is part of your family. Just as you wouldn't leave your child behind, enter this search with the attitude that you will find a place that welcomes you and your dog.

✓ Start your search as soon as you decide to move. Be realistic—don't postpone the search until a couple of weeks before your move date. Give yourself enough time to find a dog-friendly place. As a dog owner, you have the added responsibility of moving your pet as well as yourself and your family. Begin checking classified ads in the new destination's newspaper, searching the Internet, and contacting rental agencies at least six weeks before you need to move.

✓ Skip the places that clearly say "No Pets," especially large rental communities. You will only waste your time and the landlord's time in attempting to plead your case to make an exception for your corgi. Many of these places may have had bad experiences with irresponsible pet owners who have left their apartments with stained carpets and damaged walls and doors.

✓ Work on places that don't mention a pet policy in their ads, and on rentals owned by private individuals. You may be able to win over these people if you can demonstrate that you are a responsible pet parent. Let them know that you share their concerns about keeping a place clean. Emphasize that you always do "poop patrol" when you walk your dog and that you properly dispose of your pet's waste.

✓ Tap into pet-helpful resources. Contact the HSUS or an animal care and control agency serving the area to which you are moving. Many of these groups maintain current lists of apartments or condominiums that allow pets. Contact pet-owning rental agents or resident managers who share your love of animals and ask them for leads. Look in community apartment guidebooks, often available at supermarkets. At the end of this chapter we have also provided a list of pet-friendly rental Web sites you can search.

✓ Leave your dog behind—temporarily. Sometimes a new company needs you pronto, and you have to move in a hurry. If you find yourself having to live temporarily in a hotel paid for by your new company, arrange to have your dog stay with a responsible friend or family member. Once you get settled and find a dog-friendly place, your dog can join you. Work out an arrangement to pay in advance for your dog's care (food, veterinary visits, toys, etc.) so you are not creating a financial hardship on these temporary canine caregivers.

✓ Consider a temporary place. Some hotel chains offer one-bedroom suites with kitchens by the week or month, and some accept dogs. Or sign a six-month lease with an apartment complex. Either option gives you a place to call home and gives you the needed time to explore your new community and locate a more permanent, desirable place to rent.

✓ Do not try to sneak your dog into an apartment. You'll only be asking for problems. Your poor dog needs to socialize, not be kept prisoner inside a place with the drapes drawn. And the odds are strong that you will be caught, and you may be fined, evicted, or have to face other legal action.

Create a Résumé for Your Dog

Okay, you have a list of potential possibilities. Before you make that call or meet the landlord face-to-face, you still have some preparation work to do. In trying to win over a landlord, you need to sell yourself as a responsible owner and your dog as a well-mannered companion. Here are some helpful ways to wow a landlord:

- Obtain written references from former apartment owners, neighbors, pet sitters, veterinarians, and trainers who attest to your pet's good health and behavior.

- Show written proof that your dog has been spayed or neutered. Sterilized dogs exhibit far fewer behavioral problems and are less likely to be nuisances to neighbors than are intact dogs.

- Show proof that your dog is current on his vaccinations and receives regular flea treatments.

- Promise in writing to keep your dog on a leash, on a harness, or in a carrier when outside your apartment.

- Provide written documentation that your dog has aced obedience training class (or a puppy kindergarten class). Another good option: enroll your dog in the AKC's Canine Good Citizen Program.

Congratulations! You're ready to make that call or visit. If feasible, offer to bring your dog to the application interview to show the landlord how well he can sit, stay, and perform other basic commands. You also want to show how calm your dog can be. A word of advice: Provide your dog with a long, vigorous walk before the appointment so that he will be mellow.

Let's spotlight the story of Robert McClure and his wife, Sally Deneen. They decided to relocate from Fort Lauderdale, Florida, to Seattle, Washington. McClure found a terrific new job at a daily newspaper that he

---

Sample Pet Résumé

One of the most powerful new tools in your apartment hunt is a résumé. Not yours—your dog's! Bring a photo of your happy-looking dog along with his résumé when you search for apartments. Here's a sample résumé to use as a template:

Description: Freckles is a well-behaved, friendly bullmastiff, who is accustomed to apartment-life lounging and the great indoors. When he's not busy snoozing on the sofa, enjoying the sun's warming rays, he likes gazing out the window, playing nicely (and quietly) with his toys, and watching hockey with his owner. Freckles is house-trained and never messes indoors. He has been the beloved pal of Joe Smith for five years.

Health and Grooming: Freckles is neutered and flea-free. He enjoys weekly baths and regular brushing. As a preventive measure, he takes a monthly flea/tick medication. His veterinarian, Dr. I Love Dogs, rates Freckles in excellent health. Freckles is up to date on his vaccinations; medical records are provided.

Freckles's Owner: Joe Smith takes Freckles out for daily walks and properly disposes of his deposits. When Smith travels, Freckles is cared for by a professional pet sitter who also brings in the mail, waters the plants, and keeps an eye on the apartment. Joe Smith is willing to pay an extra security deposit for the privilege of having Freckles.

References: Our current landlord can be reached at 555-555-5555. Attached are letters of reference from former neighbors, our pet sitter, and our veterinarian. Also enclosed is a copy of Freckles's AKC Canine Good Citizen certificate.

couldn't turn down, and Deneen discovered that she could continue her successful freelance writing career despite being on the opposite end of the country. During their relocation trip, they had four days to find a place—one that would accept Maggie, their then 14-year-old, 55-pound German shepherd dog.

They spent the first three days feeling hopeless and rejected. They would walk into an apartment or house for rent and be part of a long line of other eager rent-seekers, all desperately charming landlords or property managers. Looking on their own in a strange new city and relying only on classified ads, they discovered that Seattle—at least on the surface—didn't exactly throw out the welcome mat to dogs in rentals. Still, they were determined. "We would never part with Maggie—she is part of our family," declared Deneen.

McClure then spotted an ad for a small house in the local community weekly. "One bedroom, bi-level, with front yard garden," the ad read. No mention of pets. They booked an appointment. When they walked up the steps, the owner greeted them— and so did her Great Dane.

They complimented the woman on the organic garden she tended in her front yard. McClure mentioned that he was an environmental reporter. Deneen asked to pet the dog and then diplomatically mentioned that the pair authored The Dog Lover's Companion to Florida book. Then she explained that they traveled throughout Florida to find hotels, beaches, and other places that permit dogs—with Maggie as their traveling companion. Deneen then sealed the deal by showing the landlord a photo of Maggie.

The story has an even happier ending. The couple eventually bought the home, and they're making sure that the garden thrives with strawberries, lettuce, peppers, and artichokes. As for Maggie, she likes to sit on the front landing and watch the neighborhood activity.

Negotiate for a Pet Lease Refund

When you do find a pet-friendly place, make sure that all agreements are made in writing. If necessary, sign a pet addendum to your rental agreement. These addendums are designed to protect people, property, and pets, too. If the lease has a no-pets clause but the landlord has verbally said okay to your dog, be sure that the clause is crossed out on both your's and your landlord's copies and initialed by both of you.

Expect to pay a pet deposit, which may or may not be refundable. And some places require that pet owners pay a little more per month. Depending on the circumstances, you may be able to negotiate for a refund—again, in writing—if at the end of the lease you can demonstrate that your dog hadn't damaged the property.

For More Details

The HSUS offers a wealth of information to renters and rental housing owners and managers. Check their Web site at www.rentwithpets.org or contact them in Washington, D.C., at (202) 452-1100. You can also find national information on renting with pets at www.peoplewithpets.com, a Web site operated by dog supporter Alex Dobrow of Woodstock, Georgia. His site is linked with the HSUS site. In the Appendix, we've provided a list of helpful Web sites to get you started on your search. Also contact your local animal shelter; many have lists of pet-friendly apartments in the area. Local humane societies also have lists of pet-friendly apartment communities in their areas and may have complete information packets as well. Good luck with your move!

Passing the Chillie Test

Mason, a 5-pound bossy Yorkshire terrier, quickly struts down the long carpeted hallway at the Pinewood Apartments in Redwood City, California. He turns his head and yaps at the loping pair of dogs 10 times his weight to get in line and follow him. *Now*. The bigger dogs do so without a fuss. In the community patio area next to the barbecue grill, Skeeter, the dachshund from apartment number 7, cools down by wading in the designated doggy pool.

Here at the 16-unit Pinewood Apartments, dogs are tenants, too. You won't find signs that read "No Pets Allowed." Manager Mary Michaels has made sure that the dogs and cats who call this place home are neutered, up to date on their shots, and flea-free, and that they play nicely with other four-legged residents. No bullies allowed.

After the customary screenings, tenants must bring their dogs to the apartment complex for the final hurdle. To gain admittance, all dogs must pass the Chillie Test. Chillie is a laid-back, blind, 12-year-old miniature poodle who shares an upstairs apartment with Michaels, along with Millie, another poodle, and Dollie, a sun-seeking, green-eyed tabby cat. Don't let Chillie's easygoing nature fool you. He takes his role as pet landlord very seriously. He's rejected a pair of snarling Afghans and permitted a 10-year-old pit bull on the condition that he become neutered.

"Okay, Chillie, let's go out the in the hallway and check out a new dog," Michaels says. Chillie stands up, stretches, does a full body shake, and strolls into the hallway. He arches his neck upward as he approaches Brittany, a 9-year-old terrier mix. The two dogs nose each other and then calmly head to the hindquarters for a healthy sniff. The introduction concludes with synchronized tail wagging. "You're in," says Michaels to Chris Wesley, owner of Brittany and two other dogs, Curly, a standard poodle, and Harmony, an Australian shepherd.

Relief sweeps over Wesley's face. "I was living in Newark, Delaware, and got this great job offer in San Jose, but I had been looking for a place for more than two months that would accept my dogs," says Wesley, an Internet application developer. "I was ready to turn down the job offer and accept a lesser position in Delaware, because I wasn't about to move without my dogs, when I heard about Chillie the pet landlord."

Pinewood Apartments is heaven on earth for dogs and cats. There are a doggy-designated pool, a monthly pet letter (which Chillie "edits"), and housewarming gifts. People get flowers. New dogs are treated to a box of biscuits and squeaky toys, and cats get soft toys they can toss. Black-and-white portraits of every four-legged tenant adorn the hallways.

The place even provides free pet sitting, including sleepovers in Michaels's apartment. When Ashley and Scott Winfrey needed to dash off for a few days on a family matter, Mason, their bossy Yorkshire terrier, insisted on sleeping under the covers in Michaels's bed. "I had Chillie on one side of the bed, Millie on the other, and Dollie had found her favorite spot," recalls Michaels with a laugh. "With Mason under the sheets by my feet, I was afraid to move a muscle all night."

Since Chillie and Michaels arrived on the scene six years ago, the place has literally gone to the dogs—and cats. Michaels says tenants stay longer and take better care of their apartments. "To be honest, I really don't want to rent to people without pets," says Michaels. "They can rent anywhere. Right, Chillie?" The poodle casts a friendly look her way and almost, as if on cue, nods.

CHAPTER 9

★ ★ ★ ★ ★ ★ ★ ★ ★ ★

PLANES, TRAINS, AUTOMOBILES, AND DOGS

★ ★ ★ ★ ★ ★ ★ ★ ★ ★

Dogs are not scampering to Department of Motor Vehicle offices demanding to take driving tests, but there is no doubt that more and more canines are hitting the road, taking to the sky, and riding the rails with their owners.

Some dogs love the adventure, the opportunity to see and sniff new places. They get to go along for the ride worry-free. But you may be surprised to learn what truly motivates people to turn their dogs into travel mates: guilt. That's right. Nearly 8 out of 10 pet owners reported that they feel guilty leaving their dogs at home when they go on a trip, according to a recent national survey conducted by the American Animal Hospital Association.

Guilt: Now you can leave home without it. Turn your feelings of frustration into fun as you and your dog take on mile after mile together. The dog-traveling trend is growing steadily, with national surveys indicating that one in every four dog owners plans vacations using pet-friendly modes of transportation and arriving at destinations that put out the canine welcome mat.

Before you book a trip, however, you need to take a few vital steps at home to ensure that your dog will enjoy the road trip and be safe. First, we recommend that you introduce your dog to the wonderful world of crates, a home within a home for dogs. By getting your dog to view the crate inside your home as a place of comfort and security, you can easily transfer these feelings when you place the crate inside your vehicle. Please refer to Chapter 4 for step-by-step guidelines on positive crate-training.

Second, take your dog for a ride—literally. Start with getting your dog used to being inside your parked car. Make the car seem like a great place by praising your dog and giving her some treats. Monitor her reaction to being inside a car. Gradually build up your dog's confidence by taking her for a ride around the block, then for a mile, and so on. Let her go with you when you need to run errands or when you want to visit a friend who lives in the next city. Your goal is to have your dog think of the car as a four-wheeled wonder—and not a direct path to a veterinary clinic where she gets poked and prodded.

Depending on the size and agreeability of your dog, you can place her inside a sturdy crate. Be sure to secure the crate to the car with a seat belt to prevent the crate from flying in a collision. Or you can attach her to a harness with a dog seat belt (available at pet supply stores).

Sure, it looks cool to have your dog as a copilot in the passenger seat with her head sticking out the window, but a free-roaming dog can get injured—or injure you—if you slam on the brakes or collide with another vehicle. A 60-pound dog who is not inside a crate or wearing a restraint belt can generate an impact force of 1,200 pounds in a 30-mph crash.

Don't let your dog stick her head out the window while you cruise along the highway. Keep the windows open a couple of inches, enough for your dog to sniff the fresh air safely and slobber on your windows. If you

Traveling with your dog can be a fun and rewarding experience.

insist on letting your dog stick her face out the passenger window, put plastic goggles over her eyes to protect them from dirt, bugs, and other flying objects. Who knows? You may start a fashion trend in your area.

Gone, too, should be the days of allowing your dog to ride in the open cab of your pickup truck. A dog in the open cab risks burning her paw pads during the hot summer months. In addition, one bump or sudden stop can send your dog airborne—causing injury and possibly costing you a fine. Dogs are banned from riding in the back of trucks in at least six states: California, Massachusetts, Maine, New Hampshire, Oregon, and Rhode Island.

Cruisin' with Your Canine

In your quest for leash-free trails, pet-friendly hotels, and dog-beckoning beaches, road trips with your dog can be fun-filled getaways for the prepared traveler.

When packing a travel bag for your dog, be sure to include her food (dry and canned), collapsible bowls for food and water, bedding, two leashes, grooming supplies, necessary medications, and a dog first aid kit. And pack plenty of spring water in resealable containers. Spring water is free from additives and chemicals and is a healthy choice to quench your canine's thirst. Other musts include cleaning supplies to handle those unexpected times your dog gets carsick or urinates in the car. Pack plenty of poop-scooping bags.

Inside your dog's traveling carrier, be sure to provide her favorite blanket and a chew toy to keep her occupied while you're driving to ease the stress of travel and make her feel at home. Keep a little water in a spill-proof dish or give your dog an ice cube to keep her hydrated.

Since traveling can be upsetting to your dog's stomach, feed her a light meal a few hours before you leave and keep feeding to a minimum during travel.

On the Road with Maggie

Maggie hears the jingling of car keys and eagerly bounds toward the door. Most times, she gets to join her owners, Sally Deneen and Robert McClure, on car trips—whether it's a trip around the block to pick up dry cleaning or a coast-to-coast move from Florida to Washington.

At last count, this 16-year-old German shepherd dog has visited 21 states—and has never gotten carsick once. She has walked The Mall, in Washington, D.C., climbing the steps of the Lincoln Memorial. She has eaten at an outdoor table of a burger joint in Austin, Texas, and she has worn cotton balls in her ears to handle the loud motor sounds aboard a Miccosukee tribe airboat ride through Florida's Everglades.

Age doesn't seem to slow her down. At 10, she made her first camping trip in a canoe, skimming the scenic waters of the Peace River in Florida. At 14, she finished her first backpacking trip in the woods of South Carolina. At 15, she pawed the sands of the remote beaches of Vancouver Island, in Canada's British Columbia. "We've always traveled with Maggie since she was a puppy," says Deneen. "We joke that Maggie has seen so much of America that she's like the Charles Kuralt of canines."

Dog Rules of the Road

✔ Make sure your dog's collar has an ID tag that lists your name and telephone number—and your veterinarian's number, if possible. Attach a travel card to your dog's carrier that includes vital information, including your dog's name, breed, color, weight, and age; your name and contact information; your veterinarian's contact number; an emergency veterinarian's contact number; and the policy name if your dog is covered by pet insurance.

✔ Identify places along the route to take rest stops. Rand McNally maps detail highway rest areas containing pet runs.

✔ Phone ahead to see for hotels that accept dogs and ask what they require for a deposit.

✔ Make sure your dog is flea-free by keeping her on a regular flea treatment program. No need for either one of you to be itching and scratching on the interstate.

✔ Keep a supply of healthy road treats in a small cooler or container. Good road chow for your dog includes apple slices, carrot sticks, air-popped popcorn (no butter), and tiny pieces of organic dog biscuits.

✔ Don't change your dog's diet. You may enjoy that greasy burger, but resist ordering one for your dog

pal. The fat and grease packed in that patty can upset her stomach and contribute to heart disease, obesity, diabetes, and a host of other ills.

✔ Keep a spray bottle of water within reach. On long, hot rides, you can spritz your dog's face and paws to cool her down.

✔ Always reattach the leash to your dog before you open the car door to prevent her from bolting out and getting lost or hit by a vehicle.

✔ Watch for excessive drooling. Drooling is a sign that your dog is starting to suffer car sickness. Park at a safe place and let her get some fresh air. Take her on a slow, gentle walk for five to ten minutes before putting her back in the car.

✔ Schedule potty breaks every two or three hours. And use the time for both of you to do a full-body stretch. Offer your dog water at every stop.

✔ Monitor the weather. Use your air-conditioning when it is warm and your heater when it is cold to prevent your dog from getting too hot or too cold.

Making the Skies Pet Friendly

More than 500,000 pets travel by airplane each year, according to the Airline Transportation Association. You can make the skies friendlier for your four-legged friend by doing some preflight planning. Here's a handy checklist:

● Select an airline-approved carrier for small dogs, usually less than 15 pounds, who can ride with you in the passenger section or an airline-approved crate for medium to large dogs who must travel in the baggage compartment. The best and safest crate is noncollapsible and made of aluminum or a plastic-aluminum combination with ample ventilation. Line the carrier with easy-to-clean materials such as newspapers or paper towels. The carrier should be big enough so that your dog can easily sit up and turn around inside it but not large enough to allow your pet to be tossed about during travel.

- Consult your veterinarian about tranquilizers or relaxing herbs if you have an anxious dog. But be careful because some breeds with short noses such as boxers and pugs are not good candidates for medications that can impair their respiratory function.

- Book early. Some airlines limit the number of pets flying in the cabin to three per flight. Reservations are made on a first-come, first-served basis.

- Select nonstop or direct flights whenever possible to avoid switching planes. Always travel on the same flight as your pet.

- Try to schedule afternoon flights during the winter and early morning or late night flights in the summer to prevent your dog from getting too cold or too hot. Be aware that many airlines impose seasonal embargoes and do not allow dogs to fly in the cargo area during extremely hot or cold days. American Airlines, for example, will not accept animals to be checked as baggage from May 15 through September 15.

- Schedule an appointment with your veterinarian within 10 days of the scheduled flight. Most airlines require up-to-date medical certificates verifying that your pet is healthy and current on all necessary vaccinations.

- Clip your dog's nails to prevent them from hooking in the crate's openings or door.

- Never remove your dog's collar with her ID tags. Some airport security personnel require dogs to be taken out of their carriers as part of a security check. You don't want your unidentified dog running through the airport. If possible, ask the security officer to scan your dog's carrier with a hand-held metal detector rather than exposing your dog to the X ray machine.

- Attach your name, address, and phone number on ID tags to your dog's collar and paste the same information on the outside of the carrier. Also provide contact information for your destination. Carry a third set of your pet's information inside your carry-on luggage.

- Write in big, bold letters at least 1 inch high, "LIVE ANIMAL" on two sides of the crate.

- Bring a current photo of your pet in case she gets lost in the airport or at the destination.

- Do not feed your pet within eight hours prior to boarding to avoid possible digestive problems during the flight. Some dogs have sensitive tummies.

- Attach an empty water dish and food dish to the inside of your dog's carrier. Fill one water tray of your dog's travel carrier with water and freeze it. Keep a day's supply of dry dog food in a sealed container in your carry-on luggage.

- Stash the leash in your purse or carry-on bag—not in the carrier or crate—to reduce the risk of your pet choking.

- Maintain a low profile during the flight with your carry-on pet, and never let her out of her carrier. Some passengers may be allergic to animal dandruff. We recommend as a courtesy that you tell the passengers next to you that you have a dog in case they are allergic so that reseating arrangements can be made with the flight attendants.

● Walk your dog just before going to the check-in gate and immediately after you land.

When booking a reservation, keep in mind that airlines differ in their policies and fees for canine travelers. Some airlines allow you to book a pet reservation as late as 24 hours in advance of a flight. Others limit the number of animals permitted inside the cabin. If you have two dogs, keep in mind that some airlines require that there be two travelers, one for each dog. Flight costs for dogs can range from $50 to $300 one way for a dog riding in the cabin

or as checked baggage, depending on the weight of the dog and crate combined.

Write down a list of questions before you contact an airline or have your travel agent book the flight: Does the airline allow all dogs or just service dogs? Does it restrict access during extreme temperatures? Do you need to travel on the same flight as your dog? Can you bring more than one dog on the plane with you? How long before scheduled departure do you need to be at the gate to check in, and does that vary based on whether the flight is domestic or international?

If you need to transport your dog and can't work out an arrangement with a commercial airline, consider contacting a professional animal shipper. The Independent Pet and Animal Transportation Association (IPATA) maintains a list of companies that specialize in transporting animals. The IPATA can be reached by telephone at (903) 769-2267, or through its Web site at www.ipata.com.

Efforts are under way to make the skies safer and friendlier for dogs. The AKC has launched a campaign against airlines that accept dogs only as cargo, which is costlier and less convenient than shipping dogs as baggage and doesn't guarantee that a dog will be on the same flight as her owner. A new federal pet air travel law has been adopted. Once compromises were made in Congress, the final version of the bill requires airlines to file monthly reports detailing incidents of an animal lost, injured, or killed while in the airline's custody. These are two good steps in the right direction to care for dogs who must travel by air.

Sherpa, the Globe-Trotting Lhasa Apso

Sherpa lives by the motto Have Bag, Will Travel. It's not unusual for her to board an airplane in New York City and land in Paris more than once a year. Sherpa's owner, Gayle Martz of New York City, makes sure Sherpa has a smooth ride. A former flight attendant and handbag designer, Martz created the Sherpa Bag, an airline-approved, HSUS-endorsed soft carrier, designed to safely tote small dogs and cats as carry-ons with their owners. "I travel constantly with my two dogs, Sherpa and Su-Nae. I love them so much," says Martz. "The carriers are like a home away from home for them." The two small dogs snooze in their carriers, tucked under the seat in front of Martz, with many passengers unaware of their presence. "My dogs have earned their flight wings, that's for sure," says Martz.

The Truth About Trains

America's trains may be some of the safest ways to travel, but they rank among the least dog-friendly modes of transportation. Amtrak, the nation's largest coast-to-coast rail system, prohibits dogs as passengers. Its policy is being challenged in a national petition campaign led by officials of the urbanhound Web site (www.urbanhound.com), a New York City-based Web site. Many local train lines do allow dogs, but there may be restrictions such as dogs must be in carriers at all times. Before you board, make sure you know the policy of the rail system on which you and your dog will be traveling.

How to Get the Greatest Enjoyment Out of Your Trip

Traveling in tandem with your dog can be exciting and can certainly help strengthen your friendship bond. But before you decide to take your dog for a ride, ask yourself these questions:

- Is this an activity that my dog will enjoy? Some shy dogs prefer being homebodies. Others leap at the chance to see the Grand Canyon or the Great Smoky Mountains.

- Is my dog well behaved? Traveling dogs should be able to sit, stay, come, leave it, and perform other actions on cue from you. Dogs who heed the rules of canine etiquette make great traveling pals and act as canine ambassadors to places that allow dogs.

- Is my dog healthy enough to make the trip? Check with your veterinarian to determine if your dog is road-ready.

You should make advance reservations at hotels along your route so that you don't pull in road-weary at midnight only to find out that your dog is not wel-

Some dogs are homebodies and don't like to travel.

come. Check the Internet or contact the American Automobile Association (AAA). The AAA publishes updated travel guides that list over 10,000 pet-friendly lodgings. Keep in mind that you should also check ahead because some hotels that were pet-accepting a year ago may have adopted strict no-pets policies now. Some require deposits or additional fees or put weight limits on pet guests. Request a room at the end of a hall and away from the ice machine or swimming pool areas to reduce the risk of your dog barking at these strange, noisy distractions.

We suggest that you not leave your dog alone in a hotel room during the first day. Let her sleep there for a night to get used to the surroundings. When you are out of your room, crate your dog so that she won't scare the hotel maid, slip out the door, or destroy the room.

Some lodgings have gone to the dogs and offer such lapdog luxuries as a "dog bar" in the lobby, a complimentary doggy bag of treats at check-in, in-room pet massages, and salons offering "peticures." These places can be found by searching the Internet and typing the key words "dog" and "spa."

If your dream is to hike a national park with your dog, call ahead and ask about the park's pet policies. Many national parks prohibit dogs on trails to protect the wildlife and their habitats. Dogs are more accepted in a park's developed area and campgrounds. Leash rules apply. So if you want to take a mule ride into the bowels of Grand Canyon National Park, keep in mind that your dog is allowed only on the trails located above the rim.

Internet Travel Aids

With the popularity of dog travel and the Internet, finding places that welcome dogs is getting easier. We offer these excellent travel guides for you:

✔ **DogGone** (www.doggonefun.com)— published six times a year, this newsletter offers fun places to go with your pet, plus savvy safety and health tips

✔ **Pets on the Go** (www.petsonthego.com)— provides tips for traveling with your dog, including money-saving suggestions and how to test your dog's suitability for travel

✔ **Petswelcome** (www.petswelcome.com)— lists dog-pleasing campgrounds, ski resorts, and beaches, as well as emergency veterinarians in the United States in case your dog needs medical attention while you are traveling

✔ **TravelDog** (www.traveldog.com)— links you to hotels in the United States and Canada that allow dogs.

It may surprise you to learn that dogs get dehydrated faster than people do. That's because they expend more energy in a short amount of time. So the higher the climb, the thirstier they will become, and the more vital it is that you take a break and give them water. And pack some munchies or kibble in a waterproof bag even if you plan to be hiking for only a couple of hours. You could accidentally get lost, and that two-hour trip could become a four-hour one. Finally, we recommend that you always pack a cell phone in case of emergency.

CHAPTER 10

★ ★ ★ ★ ★ ★ ★ ★ ★

DOGS FOR A BUSY LIFESTYLE

★ ★ ★ ★ ★ ★ ★ ★ ★

How do you pick a dog that best matches your lifestyle? The task can be more difficult than realized. Choosing a dog to adopt can be a lot of fun, yet we seem to be so bad at it. How else can we explain the millions of dogs and cats relinquished to animal shelters each year? What should be a joyous celebration of work and research all too often tends to be an expedition of first impressions and poor impulse control.

Love at first sight may seem to be a romantic way to hook up with a companion, but it rarely works well for spouse selection, and it certainly doesn't seem to work any better for selecting pets. Strange as it may sound, many people spend more time selecting a new car than they do choosing a canine companion. The critical differences between a car and a dog are that dogs live in our homes, interact with us, and often live long enough to outlast two or three new car purchases.

We'd like to help you narrow down your choices. A good place to start is by breed and their personality traits. Of course, there is really no such thing as a typical Great Dane, a usual shih tzu, or an average beagle. Each dog is an individual and deserves to be regarded as such. However, for the purposes of our activity here, we're going to rely on generalizations, stereotypes, and personal prejudices.

While there are hundreds of dogs to choose from, most of us are familiar with a few dozen breeds, so we'll try to use a small number of dogs in each category to give examples from which you can choose.

The goal is to make selection more of an objective exercise than a quest for the perfect mate.

Making the Realistic Match

Chances are that these objective criteria are important to you, even if you won't admit it. You need to take the time to make an honest assessment of yourself, your wants, your needs, your lifestyle, and your finances before you rush out and adopt a dog. Ask yourself such questions as:

- Will I make the time to take my dog for regular grooming sessions?
- Am I searching for a dog to share my daily jogs with?
- Do I abhor fur shedding on my sofa?
- Can I afford to provide food and health care for a dog?
- Am I willing to keep this dog for his entire life and meet his needs when he becomes a senior dog?

There are many factors to consider: physical features, breed, and personality traits. Let's explore some of the most critical factors together to help you determine what type of dog best complements your lifestyle.

SIZE DOES MATTER

One of the most important determinants of a dog's place in your lifestyle is size. If you live in a small apartment, you probably don't want to share it with someone who occupies more space than you do. If you're renting, whether it's a house or an apartment, landlords do consider the size of the dog who will be sharing the unit with you. Whether it is fair or not, take these factors into consideration before you acquire your dog. While it is not necessarily true that large dogs need more exercise than small ones do (we'll get to exercise requirements later), it is certainly true that large breeds cost more to feed and board, and they require more effort when you go on poop patrol. Whether you are looking for a large or small dog, choose a breed that will meet your needs based on its ultimate adult weight, not what it looks like as a puppy, the size of its paws, or how cute the fuzzy baby is. All puppies are cute. Make lifelong decisions based on what the breed is like as an adult and what you can honestly manage. Here's some information to help you size up a prospective companion.

Jack Russell terrier

Weight Ranges for Some of the More Common Breeds

20 pounds	20-40 pounds	40-80 pounds	80 pounds
Bichon fries	Basenji	Basset hound	Akita
Cairn terrier	Beagle	Boxer	Bullmastiff
Chihuahua	Brittany	Chow chow	Great Dane
Dachshund (min.)	Cocker spaniel	Collie	Irish wolfhound
Jack Russell terrier	Dachshund (std)	Dalmatian	Komondor
Lhasa apso	Finnish spitz	Doberman pinscher	Kuvasz
Miniature schnauzer	Shetland sheepdog	English springer spaniel	Mastiff
poodle (min)	Welsh corgi	Golden retriever	Newfoundland
Pug	Whippet	Old English sheepdog	Rottweiler
Shih tzu	Soft-coated wheaten terrier	Samoyed	Saint Bernard

NO BARKING ZONE

Barking is a subjective characteristic but can have profound influences on your living situation. Ideally, most people want a dog who barks fero-ciously when someone undesirable approaches their home. At the same time, they want a dog who is silent the rest of the time. If a dog barks all day long while you are away at work, expect that you will not be popular in your immediate neighborhood.

Proper socialization is important in preventing your dog from stressing out and barking while you are not home, but there are some breed tendencies that you can consider, depending on your individual requirements. Remember, these are just generaliza-tions. If you get a basenji and she turns out to be a howler, don't blame us! We're just offering suggestions.

Low Tendency to Bark	High Tendency to Bark
Afghan	Beagle
Basenji	Bichon fries
Boxer	Cairn terrier
Brittany	Dachshund
Bull terrier	Hounds (all types)
Cocker spaniel	Lhasa apso
Greyhound	Miniature schnauzer
Leonberger	Pomeranian
Newfoundland	Shih tzu
Saluki	Yorkshire terrier

Dachshund

TENDENCY TO DROOL

Drooling is another subjective category, primarily based on the anatomic features of the dog's lips and whether or not they tend to pool saliva. Some dogs just tend to slobber regardless of their lip confor-mation. If you're a neat freak and don't like the

Low Tendency to Drool	High Tendency to Drool
Beagle	Basset hound
Border collie	Bloodhound
Chihuahua	Boxer
Cocker spaniel	Bullmastiff
Dachshund	Clumber spaniel
Jack Russell terrier	English setter
Labrador retriever	Great Dane
Poodle	Mastiff
Shih tzu	Newfoundland
Welsh corgi	Saint Bernard

concept of salivary streams on most of your wardrobe, this is a factor that could definitely affect your relationship with your pooch. Don't blame the dog! Chances are you selected him for those lips in the first place.

Most owners who learn to love drooling dogs favor bandanas, which can be used for quick mop-ups, and strategically placed cloths or diapers that can be used for greater fluid accumulations. Here are a few breeds that have gained notoriety for their propensity to drool. If this is a make-or-break quality for your proposed compan- ion, take heed.

Bulldog

ODD BEDFELLOWS

If you're like many on-the-go dog owners, chances are you'll be sharing your bed with your furry com- panion. On top of the usual debates about which side of the bed to give up and personal hygiene issues is whether you can handle it if your new bedmate snores. This is also a subjective assessment, but you can often identify a potential snorer by breed, based on the anatomic features of the throat, and to a cer- tain extent on obesity.

Many brachycephalic breeds, those with pushed- in faces, have compressed breathing passages and are destined to snore. Other dogs may snore for no apparent reason, regardless of the breed-related conformation. Take this following list as a guide only, but here are our top 10 snoring serenaders for you to consider in your selection process.

Low Tendency to Snore	High Tendency to Snore
Afghan hound	Affenpinscher
Cairn terrier	Basset hound
Collie	Boxer
Greyhound	Bullmastiff
Jack Russell terrier	Clumber spaniel
Miniature pinscher	English bulldog
Miniature poodle	French bulldog
Papillon	Great Dane
Saluki	Pekingese
Shetland sheepdog	Pug

TENDENCY TO DIG

If you consider your yard and garden to be objects of beauty and sanctuaries for your senses, you probably won't appreciate your new companion bulldozing your freshly placed sod or ripened cherry tomatoes in a search for hidden treasures. Some breeds just seem to have a propensity to dig, but any breed can damage your property by digging, either because of innate behavior or in an attempt to tunnel out to escape. Once again, there are no guarantees about breed selection and digging, but we're going to venture forth with some recommendations anyway.

EXERCISE REQUIREMENTS

This is the make-or-break condition for many new dog owners. They get a golden retriever because they want to start a new exercise kick and are amazed that when they've decided that exercise is overrated and inactivity is a virtue, the

Low Tendency to Dig	High Tendency to Dig
Basenji	Airedale
Basset hound	Akita
Bichon frise	Beagle
Bloodhound	Boston terrier
Borzoi	Cairn terrier
Bullmastiff	Chow chow
Cavalier King Charles spaniel	English springer spaniel
Greyhound	Finnish spitz
Lhasa apso	Keeshond
Maltese	Siberian husky

Some General Exercise Times for Breeds	
20 Minutes of Exercise Each Day	40 Minutes of Exercise Each Day
Basset hound	Airedale
Boston terrier	Akita
Chihuahua	Brittany
Chow chow	Collie
Lhasa apso	Dalmatian
Maltese	German shepherd dog
Mastiff	Golden retriever
Pekingese	Irish setter
Pug	Labrador retriever
Yorkshire terrier	Rottweiler

Airedale terrier

German shepherd dog

dog still demands activity. How could that dog be so insensitive!

If you select a dog who has exercise requirements greater than your own, problems will ensue. And don't assume that eventually your new pet will decide that he really doesn't need activity after all. Many dogs who are denied the exercise they crave will develop behavioral problems to signal owners that everything is not okay in their lives. Listen to that message or you are likely to come home to find your couch serving as an appetizer for your frustrated furry friend.

But don't just assume that a working dog such as a greyhound needs excessive exercise. Most greyhounds, even ones retired from the track, make great couch potatoes and can be very happy with a sedentary lifestyle. Your job is to determine your exercise match before you take a dog into your life, not after.

If you've adopted a dog with abundant energy and the need for exercise, don't fret. Seek out a friend who likes to jog and see if he or she would like a running companion who could serve double duty as security. If all else fails, and you can't bear to exercise yourself, consider teaching your dog to retrieve a flying disc and let him do all the real work. You concentrate on conserving your energy, flinging the disc for your dog to fetch, and keeping your eyes open for members of the opposite sex who are taking an active interest. There's always an upside to taking your pet to public areas!

NEED FOR ATTENTION

Some people need to be needed, and this is often reflected in the time they spend with their pets. Other people would rather lead active social lives that don't involve their pets. Whatever your preference, remember that all dogs are social creatures, but they do vary considerably in the demands they put on your time.

If you work all day and party all night, you may want to reconsider why you wanted a dog in the first place. Most dogs, however, can get along fine without you for considerable periods of time, as long as you take their needs into consideration. We've made some generalizations about breeds, but if you are reasonable, just about any dog can adjust to your schedule.

Low Social Attention Needs	High Social Attention Needs
Afghan hound	Bichon frise
Bloodhound	Boston terrier
Chow chow	Chihuahua
Curly-coated retriever	Cocker spaniel
Field spaniel	Dalmatian
Finnish spitz	Lhasa apso
Ibizan hound	Shih tzu
Kuvasz	Silky terrier
Komondor	Whippet
Siberian husky	Yorkshire terrier

Yorkshire terrier

IT'S A FUR THING

Everyone appreciates a nice head of hair, but keeping it looking great is sometimes more work than one can handle. You can imagine how much work grooming would be if your entire body were covered with hair and you tended to drag it around on the ground wherever you went. The fact is that some breeds have quite elaborate grooming requirements while others are more the wash-and-go variety.

Viszla

Low Grooming Requirements	High Grooming Requirements
Basenji	Afghan hound
Boxer	Cocker spaniel
Chihuahua	Collie
Dalmatian	Golden retriever
Doberman pinscher	Irish setter
Great Dane	Lhasa apso
Greyhound	Old English sheepdog
Labrador retriever	Pekingese
Viszla	Shih tzu
Weimaraner	Silky terrier
Whippet	Yorkshire terrier

Now, if you have your heart set on an Afghan hound, there are grooming cuts that make the fur easier to manage, but the dog might not look like the breed you fell in love with. Just expect that if you want that long, flowing mane, it's going to take work and the skills of a professional dog groomer. You'll need to factor in time and money for breeds with hairy needs. Just as long as you're realistic, you'll both be happy.

OKAY, I CAN HANDLE THE GROOMING AS LONG AS THEY DON'T SHED!

Unless you are selecting a bald breed, expect that most dogs are going to shed, at least some. After all, you shed, so why shouldn't your canine companion? If you are concerned about unsightly collections of fur around your living area, you might want to take our advice on breed selection, brush regularly to remove fur, and limit exposure to pieces of furniture that are beyond compromise. Drape a cot-

Soft-coated wheaten terrier

Low Tendency to Shed	High Tendency to Shed
Affenpinscher	Akita
Bichon frise	American Eskimo dog
Chinese crested	Bearded collie
Italian greyhound	Belgian sheepdog
Miniature schnauzer	Collie
Poodle	German shepherd dog
Puli	Golden retriever
Wire fox terrier	Malamute
Xoloitzcuintli	Siberian husky
Soft-coated wheaten terrier	Labrador retriever

ton sheet over your furniture to keep fur adherence to a minimum, but also keep sticky tape and a lint brush handy if you or your guests are sensitive to misplaced fur.

HELP! I'M SENSITIVE

No dogs are entirely nonallergenic, but it is possible to own a dog even if you have a documented sensitivity. The most important factor is to select a breed that is considered less allergenic than others. Test your reaction before bringing the dog home. Once home, have someone (not you) routinely wipe the dog down with solutions that will help remove fur and dander before you have the opportunity to inhale them. These solutions are commercially available, but water is an acceptable alternative in many cases.

Remember, too, that dogs often collect considerable amounts of pollen and mold in their coats when they go outdoors. If you have sensitivities to these items as well, make wiping the dog down a routine event whenever your dog comes in from the great outdoors. It may not be possible to completely eliminate hypersensitivities in this manner, but we certainly understand the motivation for wanting to give it a try. It is a good idea for people with allergies/pollen sensitivities to "clear the air" by placing HEPA filters in key rooms of the house, especially bedrooms and living rooms. And train your dog to go into a crate or his own dog bed outside of your bedroom to keep allergens from accumulating in the bedroom.

Breeds with Lower Allergenicity

- Bedlington terrier
- Bichon frise
- Bouvier des Flandres
- Irish water spaniel
- Miniature schnauzer
- Old English sheepdog
- Pharaoh hound
- Poodle
- Portuguese water dog

Miniature schnauzer

Behavioral Personality Testing

Okay, it sounds more like a computer dating service than a dog selection device, but don't underestimate the value of making sure that you and your fur-faced friend are compatible before you say "I do." Veterinary behaviorists are available if you run into trouble, but do yourself a big favor and start paying attention to those little habits that you find annoying (such as being repeatedly nipped on the ankles), and take action before they become permanent traits. After all, dating is about getting to know someone before you get too serious about them. Why should selecting a dog companion be any different? Keep in mind that most dogs will live with you for 10 years or more. These days, a dog's life span may last longer than a marriage. Behavioral tests are much more accurate when conducted on a full-grown dog than on a puppy. If you don't mind adopting an adult dog, you can probably deter most of his bad habits in a relatively short span of time. If the dog tries to bite you, that is definitely a bad sign. Puppies may play bite, but an older dog who tries to hurt you is a problem to be avoided. This is no time to be codependent or wanting to adopt the problem dog at the shelter to make yourself look like a hero. With your on-the-go lifestyle, you need a confident, friendly dog who is as sociable as you are.

Personality testing, whether done on a puppy or an adult dog, really means documenting that you are the boss in this human-canine relationship. Being the boss doesn't mean that you have to bark out orders to your dog every few minutes. But it does mean that your dog must respect your authority and recognize you as the top dog in the household. Dogs are pack animals who are used to functioning in a social hierarchy. If you want to earn your dog's respect, you must be dominant (not domineering) and consistent with your household rules. This is not an association of equals.

Okay, enough lecturing about dominance. To test a dog's personality, you want to demonstrate that the dog is interested in you (endless devotion will follow) and that there are no displays of unwanted behaviors such as being overly fearful or aggressive. When you first meet a potential candidate, notice if the dog prefers to spend time with you more than with other dogs. If so, this is a good sign. Then take the dog away from other dogs, people, and distractions and observe how the two of you interact. Expect that the dog will first spend a brief time exploring the surroundings but then should want to spend some quality time playing with you. This is a sure sign that the dog is sociable.

Now comes the tough part. You need to see if the dog will respect your authority. The easiest way to test for this is to bring along some grooming instruments. Try brushing the dog's coat. Brush all around the head, the hind end, and even the belly. Then handle the toes on all feet. Look to see how clean the toes and foot pads are. Take a cotton swab and gently wipe along the outer opening of the ear. If the dog is being receptive, consider lifting his upper lip to examine the condition of his teeth. But if at any time you feel that you are placing yourself at risk of being bitten, stop immediately!

Please do not adopt any dog who demonstrates aggression toward you while you are doing these routine handling actions. Young puppies may nip because they have yet to learn bite inhibition, but an adult dog who shows any inclination of intent to hurt you is not acceptable. By the same token, any dog who is overly submissive or who urinates when you touch him is probably not a good choice either. This dog may be too fearful or suffer from severe separation anxiety.

Keep in mind that you need to be highly selective when choosing a dog. Fortunately, there are plenty of friendly, tail-wagging dogs available who would leap at the chance of landing a good home.

We've placed a lot of emphasis in this chapter on the selection process because we feel it is imperative to pick the right dog to complement your busy lifestyle. We implore you to select a dog who suits your lifestyle and to train him to be your lifelong companion. Neither of you will be disappointed with the results.

Before you adopt a dog be sure to do a behavioral test.

CHAPTER 11

* * * * * * * * * *

PUTTING YOUR DOG
UP FOR ADOPTION

* * * * * * * * * *

The day you hoped would never arrive has. Despite all your best intentions, it is just no longer possible for you and your dog to share a home. Divorce, a family death, an illness, relocation, or chronic canine misbehaviors commonly top the list of reasons a family dog must be relinquished to an animal shelter, rescue group, pet sanctuary, or friend. Whatever the reason, the decision is emotionally draining and trying. You may feel that you've failed as a pet parent. Since this book is about parenting a dog without guilt, we're going to do what we can to help you through this tough situation. But first, we need to describe why people face problems when they need to give up their dogs.

Pet overpopulation continues to be a major problem across the country. Currently there are millions of dogs with homes in the United States, and it is likely that millions more are without this luxury. While the number of household pets has stabilized, for the most part, the number of homeless animals is rising, and millions of these animals are killed each year.

We are now in the twenty-first century, and despite major advances in veterinary medicine and the firm commitment of animal control agencies and pet advocates, we have made little progress toward a solution to the pet overpopulation problem. It is estimated that 5,500 dogs and cats are born each hour in this country, yet the total number of pets within households is growing slowly. It is also estimated that more than eleven million animals per year are taken into the 6,400 shelters located across the country and that approximately two-thirds of pets entering an animal shelter will never leave; only one-third of animals in shelters are adopted or reclaimed by their owners.

Statistics released by the National Council on Pet Population Study and Policy (NCPPSP) reveal that only 16 percent of dogs entering animal shelters are ever reclaimed by their owners; more than 25 percent are adopted out to other families, and more than 56 percent are euthanized. It's not that shelters want to kill these animals, but the number of animals processed is truly incredible. By some estimates, between ten and twenty million dogs and cats are killed at the country's shelters each year. This means that more than 15 percent of the entire dog population in the United States is killed each year, and those numbers are climbing.

Every shelter in the country would prefer to be a no-kill shelter, but many do not have the space or the funding to be able to keep and provide care to their orphaned dogs for an indefinite period of time. There simply are millions more dogs who need homes than there are homes that want dogs.

Don't despair. The intent of this chapter is to help you find a guilt-free way of relocating your canine companion. We provided the sad statistics to demonstrate what can happen when you aren't prepared to deal with the situation responsibly. When you split up with a spouse or a significant other, you each have emotional wounds to heal. But when you surrender a dog to the system, the impact may be more jarring—a possible death sentence to your dog. Let's make sure that doesn't happen.

Training

If you have invested your time and energy into your relationship with your dog, especially in the form of training, you will likely have no problems whatsoever finding a home for your furry friend. A well-mannered dog is a joy to behold and phenomenally adoptable. Our experience is that if you travel just about anywhere with a well-socialized dog, people will approach you about where they could find such a dog. If you've done your job and have been a good parent to your pooch, you needn't worry about finding a good home—potential owners will be seeking you out.

In our opinion, putting your energies into training and socializing your dog is the most important thing you can do to make your pooch a desirable adoptee. If you and Maggie have completed the AKC's Canine Good Citizen Program, your dog will be very desirable indeed.

Health Care

Next to training, health care is the most important aspect of making a dog adoptable. A dog who is neutered or spayed, current on her vaccinations, and well cared for is a real bonus for anyone looking for a dog. Many people who don't have the time—or the patience—to house-train a puppy are more attracted to a mature adult dog who comes to them healthy and trained. If you offer to extend the dog's health insurance policy for a year, potential owners have a kind of warranty in case your dog has medical needs that you, or they, never anticipated. This action may give you some peace of mind, assuring that if something happens to your dog, she will be cared for.

All too often, when people are searching the classified ads or bulletin boards for their next dog, vital information such as the health of the dog and her training is either unavailable or incomplete. Worse yet, some pet advertisers may purposefully withhold the information so they can unload their problematic animals on unsuspecting, but hopefully kind-hearted, individuals. If you can provide medical records from your veterinarian and a recent veterinary note about your dog's good health (such as the kind issued by veterinarians for pets crossing borders), you are miles ahead of the competition.

Putting this information into a nice file completes the package for the perfect dog who needs a home. Just imagine such a packet that includes a complete health record documenting all veterinary care (the next owner will need this information for licensing, boarding, crossing borders, etc.), together with perhaps a Canine Good Citizen diploma, insurance policy, and letter of reference from a landlord or boarding facility. If you have registry papers for a purebred, these should be included as well. In essence, you're preparing a portfolio for your dog in hopes of landing her not a new job but a new home. What could be better?

One final touch: we recommend that you include a one-page summary of your dog's personality pluses and accomplishments, together with her favorite activities, the diet that you have been feeding her, commands to which your dog responds, and any routines that have been established. Be honest. If your dog prefers to be the only pet in the house, say so. If your dog has a high-energy drive, let prospective adopters know. In finding a new home for your dog, there should be no surprises to members of her new home. Remember that parting will be stressful for both of you, and providing this information to the next owner will make the transition smoother for all.

The best source for new owners is your current network of pet allies, including your veterinary hospital, boarding facility, groomer, dog walker, pet sitter, and dog trainer. Rank these people as your priority group in helping you find the right new home for your dog. These people make their living working with animals and possess a much broader network of contacts for current and prospective dog owners than your well-meaning friends, family, and colleagues. Rank these people in your second tier in helping place your dog.

If you originally got your dog from a professional licensed breeder, contact him or her. Let the breeder know of your situation. Often breeders know someone who would like an adult dog from one of their lines. Anyone who knows what a great catch your dog is can likely identify several other people who would love to bring such a dog into their lives. Remember the old saying, It's Not What You Know, But Who You Know!

Many responsible breed organizations have members who also serve as rescue people for surrendered pedigreed dogs. They'll gladly temporarily place a dog in a foster home until a match can be found. And you can feel better knowing that your dog's future home will be with a person or family who really likes and knows the unique personalities and needs of her specific breed.

More than 130 AKC breeds have rescue service contacts listed on the AKC Web site (www.akc.org). Rescue groups can act as vital matchmakers between a dog in need of a home and a potential owner looking for a particular breed. Some also temporarily house these dogs to hone their socialization skills with people and other pets to increase their adoptability. They also are excellent at screening out unsuitable "suitors" for your dog. They check references of prospective owners and do follow-up visits to check on the dog's welfare.

If you are not fortunate enough to come across suitable individuals to adopt your dog, the next step is to contact the shelters in your area, not to relinquish your pet but to identify potential adoptive owners and foster families in your area. Shelters will be listed in your telephone book, but most of the other services will not.

Questions to Ask Prospective Adopters

Resist handing your dog over to the first interested person. To help you select the right new owner, obtain answers to the following questions during your interview:

✔ Why do you want to adopt this dog?

✔ Have you ever owned a dog as an adult before, and, if so, have you owned a dog of this breed?

✔ Do you own or rent? If you rent, please provide contact information for your landlord so that I can verify that pets are accepted.

✔ Do you have a yard? Is it fenced?

✔ Do you live near a dog-friendly park or other safe place to walk your dog?

✔ What other pets to you have, and do they get along with other dogs?

✔ Who else lives with you? Do you have any children—if so, how many and what are their ages?

✔ Who will be primarily responsible for caring for this dog?

✔ What type of training methods do you use on a dog?

✔ Where will the dog live? Inside or outside?

✔ Do you travel a lot? If so, what provisions will you make to care for your dog while you're away?

✔ What type of activities and exercises do you want to do with this dog?

✔ If you already have a veterinarian, would you mind letting me contact him or her for a reference?

✔ What's your daily routine like during the workweek and during weekends?

It may seem that such questioning would deter an individual from adopting your dog, but you need to look at the big picture. If this dog actually means something to you, you want to be assured that six months from now, after all your hard work, your pooch doesn't end up in a shelter because of a mismatch that could have been avoided.

You can also find information on shelters, rescue organizations, and foster programs on the Internet, and we've provided some links in Appendix B. The goal is to tap into the existing networks that have been established to place animals in appropriate homes.

If you aren't having any success, consider placing classified ads in your local newspaper, and don't overlook the power of your community weekly. Post your need to find your dog a new home on community bulletin boards at your supermarket, veterinary office, pet supply stores, and other high-traffic places. We caution you, however, that the biggest danger of these approaches is that people who get their pets from such sources are often the most uninformed about pet care. They are typically the ones who are impressed with papers and tales about pedigrees, and may not want their pet to be neutered because they hoped to breed him or her for fun and profit. Many others are first-time dog owners and may not even have a good idea about what is involved in raising a dog. There's no doubt that many of these individuals have big hearts and would welcome your fun-loving dog into their lives, but they are infinitely harder to screen than are individuals identified by pet allies such as breeders or your veterinarian.

If you are going to place an ad, never use the words free to *a good home*. You don't want to lure bargain shoppers; you want to attract responsible dog owners. Attach a price to your dog, say $100. This is not to make money off your dog but to filter out people who cannot afford this amount of money. If a person can't pay for a dog, how can he or she afford routine or emergency veterinary care? The amount you charge could be the annual premium of the insurance policy you are providing.

Be a little creative and play up your dog's pluses to catch the attention of the right prospective owner. Better to write an ad that emphasizes your dog's positive traits. Maybe she is an AKC Canine Good Citizen, can fetch the television remote control, or likes to dance competitively and is in need of a new partner. If possible, provide an adorable photo of your dog, too. These tactics will sell your dog's strengths much better than a plain ad that only cites breed and availability of papers. You'll attract an entirely different sort of canine connoisseur.

In the end, finding a new owner for your dog is kind of like hiring someone for a position in your company. The individual who is recommended to you by someone you know and trust and who comes prepared to provide credentials and references is almost always going to be a better bet than someone who cold-calls you, doesn't really know what the job entails, and hasn't bothered to put together a résumé and references. Either candidate may be a wonderful employee, but you'll certainly sleep better if you select the former rather than the latter. The same goes for dog selection, so make it work for you!

Shelters and humane societies are the final chance to find a new home for your pooch if all else fails. The main problem is that, in many cases, when you relinquish your pet, you lose the ability to select the new owner, and your dog's fate is decidedly uncertain. You give up all rights—including being informed if your dog was adopted or euthanized. You need to recognize and accept this before you bring your dog into a shelter.

As mentioned previously, no-kill shelters are available. All shelters wish that they could offer this service, but it would be impossible for all shelters to be no-kill and still house all the animals who need homes. It's a sad state of events, but it's reality. All the more reason to plan ahead for a smooth and relatively uneventful transition to your dog's new home. Best of luck to both of you!

As a quick summary, let's recap the key points:

- Dogs sleep up to 17 hours a day, including while they are home alone and you are at work.
- Never make a big deal out of leaving or entering your home to reduce the chance of your dog developing separation anxiety.
- Provide mental and physical outlets for your dog on a daily basis. A tired dog is a happy dog. Give

The quality time that you spend with your dog is what matters most.

your dog durable chew toys and hollow hard rubber toys stuffed with food to keep him occupied while you're away.

- Shop for dog-friendly products such as room gates, and doggy crates that can safely confine your dog to limited areas of your home while you're away.
- Tap pet-friendly allies such as dog-friendly bosses, dog walkers, pet sitters, doggy day care operators, and veterinarians and groomers who make house calls.
- Be prepared for a natural disaster by keeping an identification tag on your dog's collar coupled with a microchipped ID.
- Encourage good behavior and work in mini-

training sessions to hone your dog's obedience skills. Key commands: *leave it*, *sit*, *come*, and *stay*.

- Develop a pet resume you can present to landlords when apartment hunting and negotiate for a pet lease refund if you leave the apartment in good condition.
- Sharing the responsibility of caring for you dog with all members of the household, including your children.

Congratulations! You're learned to take the G-U-I-L-T out of sharing your life with a canine pal. And, you've recognized that it is not the amount of time but the quality of time spent that matters most in fostering a happy, healthy relationship between you and your dog.

Appendix A

* * * * * * * * *

HELPFUL ADDRESSES

* * * * * * * * *

American Animal Hospital Association
P.O. Box 150899
Denver, CO 80215
(800) 252-2242

American Holistic Veterinary Medical Association
2218 Old Emmorton Road
Bel Air, MD 21015
(410) 569-0795

American Humane Association
63 Inverness Drive East
Englewood, CO 80112
(800) 227-4645

American Kennel Club
5580 Centerview Drive
Raleigh, NC 27606
(919) 233-9767

American Veterinary Medical Association
1931 North Meacham Road, Suite 100
Schaumburg, IL 60173
(847) 925-8070

The Anti-Cruelty Society
157 West Grand Avenue
Chicago, IL 60610
(312) 644-8338

ASPCA/National Animal Poison Control Center
2001 South Lincoln Avenue
Urbana, Ill.
(888) 426-4435

Canine Resource and Referral Helpline
Sponsored by the American Dog Trainers Network
(212) 727-7257

Delta Society

580 Naches Ave. SW Suite 101

Renton, WA 98055

(800) 869-6898

Humane Society of the United States

2100 L Street, NW

Washington, DC 20037

(202) 452-1100

Check the HSUS pet-friendly landlord site at

www.rentwithpets.org

Lost and Found Hotline for Pets

For a minor per-minute fee, they will help people who have lost pets. (900) 535-1515. To report a found pet, call toll-free (800) 755-8111.

Morris Animal Foundation

45 Inverness Drive East

Englewood, CO 80112

(800) 243-2345

PetFinders

(800) 666-5678

Pet Sitters International

201 East King Street

King, NC 27021

(336) 983-9222

Appendix B

★ ★ ★ ★ ★ ★ ★ ★ ★

INTERNET RESOURCES

★ ★ ★ ★ ★ ★ ★ ★ ★

The Internet provides a wealth of information for dog owners, but by its very nature, the content can get outdated as new players enter the field while other players depart. This is the most current information available, but it is not timeless. Most of the information has been gleaned from *Dr. Ackerman's Veterinary Guide to the Internet* ©2003 and is reprinted with permission.

Activities

AKC Agility Association	www.akc.org/dic/events/agility/index.cfm
American Mixed Breed Obedience Registration	www.amborusa.org
Bright and Beautiful Therapy Dogs Inc.	www.golden-dogs.org
Canine Good Citizen	www.akc.org/love/cgc/index.cfm
Canine Water Sports	www.caninewatersports.com
Dog-Play	www.dog-play.com
Flyball	www.flyballdogs.com/flyball.html
Frisbee	www.dogpatch.org/dogs/frisbee.cfm
North American Dog Agility Council	www.nadac.com
North American Flyball Association	www.flyball.org
Scootering	www.dogscooter.com
Skijoring	www.skijorama.com
Therapy Dogs International	www.tdi-dog.org
United Kennel Club	www.ukcdogs.com
US Dog Agility Association	www.usdaa.com
US Disc Dog Nationals	www.discdog.org
World Canine Freestyle Organization	www.worldcaninefreestyle.org

Animal Registries

American Kennel Club	www.akc.org
American Rare Breed Association	www.arba.org
Canadian Kennel Club	www.ckc.ca
Fédération Cynologique Internationale FCI	www.fci.be
The Kennel Club	www.the-kennel-club.org.uk
United Kennel Club	www.ukcdogs.com

Animal Welfare Sites

American Humane	www.amerhumane.org
American Pet Association	www.apapets.com
American SPCA	www.aspca.org
Anti-Cruelty Society	www.anticruelty.org
The Humane Society of the United States	www.hsus.org

Gadgets and Gizmos

Hot Diggity Dog (Collectables)	www.hotdiggitydog.com
K9 Gifts (Collectables)	www.k9gifts.com
MD Pet Music	www.mdpetmusic.com
Pet Safe (Health and Behavior Products)	www.petsafe.net
Puttin' on the Dog (Collectables)	www.puttinonthedog.com
Red Dog Designs (Collectables)	www.reddogdesigns.com
Three Dog Bakery (Bakery and Accessories)	www.threedog.com

Magazine Sites

Dog Fancy	www.dogfancy.com
Dog World	www.dogworldmag.com
Dogs USA	www.animalnetwork.com/usa/dusadefault.asp
Puppies USA	www.animalnetwork.com

National Apartment Locators

ApartmentGuide.com	www.apartmentguide.com
Apartments.com	www.apartments.com
ApartmentWorld.com	www.apartmentworld.com
ForRent.com	www.forrent.com
PeopleWithPets.com	www.peoplewithpets.com
PetApartments.net	www.petapartments.net
Homestore.com	www.springstreet.com

Pet Food Sites

DLM Foods L.L.C.	www.heinzpet.com
Hill's Pet Nutrition	www.hillspet.com
Iams	www.iams.com
Kal Kan (Mars Incorporated)	www.kalkan.com
Nestle Purina PetCare USA	www.purina.com
Waltham	www.waltham.com

Pet Insurance Companies and Other Plans

CareCredit	www.carecredit.com
PetAssure	www.petassure.com
Pet Care Insurance	www.petcareinsurance.com
Petshealth Care Plan	www.petshealthplan.com
Premier Pet Insurance	www.ppins.com
Veterinary Pet Insurance	www.petinsurance.com

Rescue Organizations

AKC National Breed Club Rescue	www.akc.org/breeds/rescue.cfm
Pets Unlimited	www.petsunlimited.com
The Poop	www.thepoop.com/search_rescue.asp

Service Organizations

American Boarding Kennels Association	www.abka.com
American Dog Trainers Network	www.inch.com/~dogs
Association of Pet Behaviour Counsellors	www.apbc.org.uk
Association of Professional Dog Trainers	www.apdt.com
International Association of Pet Cemeteries	www.iaopc.com/home.htm
National Association of Professional Pet Sitters	www.petsitters.com
Pet Club of America	www.petclub.org
Pet Shelters	www.petshelter.org
Pet Sitters International	www.petsit.com

Sites Dealing with Health Issues

American Animal Hospital Association	www.healthypet.com
American Association of House call Veterinarians	www.athomevet.org
American Veterinary Medical Association	www.avma.org
Canine Eye Registry Foundation (CERF)	www.vmdb.org/cerf.html

Institute for Genetic Disease Control (GDC)	www.vetmed.ucdavis.edu/gdc/gdc.html
Morris Animal Foundation	www.MorrisAnimalFoundation.org
National Animal Poison Control Center	www.aspca.org/apcc
Orthopedic Foundation for Animals	www.offa.org

Sites to Help You Select a Breed

American Kennel Club	www.akc.org/breeds
Digital Dogs	www.digitaldog.com/breeds.html
K9Web	www.k9web.com/dog-faqs/breeds/
Purina	www.purina.com
United Kennel Club	www.ukcdogs.com/breeds.htm

Travel Directories

Dog Camps	www.dogpatch.org/doginfo/camp.html
Dog Friendly	www.dogfriendly.com
Dog Parks	www.dogpark.com
Independent Pet and Animal Transportation Association	www.ipata.com
InnSeeker.com	www.innseekers.com/pet.cfm
Hike with Your Dog	www.hikewithyourdog.com
Hot Dog Holidays	www.hotdogholidays.com
Pets on the Go	www.petsonthego.com
Petswelcome	www.petswelcome.com
PetTravel	www.pettravel.com
TravelDog	www.traveldog.com
Travel Pets	www.travelpets.com

Working Dog Sites

Canine Companions for Independence	www.caninecompanions.org
Delta Society	www.deltasociety.org
Guide Dogs	www.guidedogs.org

Appendix C

★ ★ ★ ★ ★ ★ ★ ★ ★

BIBLIOGRAPHY

★ ★ ★ ★ ★ ★ ★ ★ ★

Ackerman, Lowell. *Dr. Ackerman's Veterinary Guide to the Internet.* Mass.: Lowell Ackerman, 2003.

——. *The Contented Canine: A Guide to Successful Pet Parenting for Dog Owners.* Lincoln, Nebr.: ASJA Press, 2001.

American Animal Hospital Association. "American Animal Hospital Association 11th Annual Pet Owner Survey," *American Animal Hospital Association* (2002).

Ascione, Frank R., Ph.D. "Safe Havens for Pets: Guidelines for Programs Sheltering Pets for Women Who Are Battered," *The Geraldine R. Dodge Foundation* (2000).

Beck, Alan M. *Between Pets and People: The Importance of Animal Companionship.* Ashland, Ohio: Purdue University Press, 1996.

Friedmann, E., and Thomas, S.A. "Pet Ownership, Social Support, and One Year Survival after Acute Myocardial infarction in the Cardiac Arrhythmia Suppression Trial (CAST)," *American Journal of Cardiology* 76 (1995): 1213.

Lachman, Larry and Mickadeit, Frand. *Dogs on the Couch: Behavior Therapy for Training and Caring for Your Dog.* New York: Overlook Press, 1999.

Long, Lynette and Thomas G. *The Handbook for Latchkey Children and Their Parents.* New York: Berkley Publishing Group, 1984.

Lovern, Cindy S., D.V.M. "Saving the Whole Family," *American Veterinary Medical Association* (2002).

MetLife. "MetLife Study of Employee Benefits Trends," *MetLife* (2001).

Moore, Arden. *Dog Training, a Lifelong Guide.* Irvine, Calif.: BowTie Press, 2002

——. *50 Simple Ways to Pamper Your Dog.* Mass.: Storey Books, 2000.

——. *Real Food for Dogs.* Mass.: Storey Books, 2001.

Ryan, Terry. *The Toolbox for Remodeling Your Problem Dog.* New York: Hungry Minds, 1998.

Wise, Stephen W. and Goodall, Jane. *Rattling the Cage: Toward Legal Rights for Animals.* Oxford, U.K.: Perseus Press, 2000.